T0109304

KISS MY
CASSEROLE!

KISS MY CASSEROLE!

100 MOUTHWATERING RECIPES INSPIRED BY OVENS AROUND THE WORLD

HOWIE SOUTHWORTH and GREG MATZA

Skyhorse Publishing

Skyhorse Publishing books may be purchased in bulk at special discounts for sales promotion, corporate gifts, fund-raising, or educational purposes. Special editions can also be created to specifications. For details, contact the Special Sales Department, Skyhorse Publishing, 307 West 36th Street, 11th Floor, New York, NY 10018 or info@skyhorsepublishing.com.

Visit our website at www.skyhorsepublishing.com.

10 9 8 7 6 5 4 3

Library of Congress Cataloging-in-Publication Data

Names: Southworth, Howie, author. | Matza, Greg, author.
Title: Kiss my casserole! : 100 mouthwatering recipes inspired by ovens around the world / Howie Southworth and Greg Matza.
Description: New York : Skyhorse Publishing, [2018]
Identifiers: LCCN 2017042269| ISBN 9781510728141 (hardcover : alk. paper) | ISBN 9781510728165 (ebook)
Subjects: LCSH: Casserole cooking. | Comfort food. | LCGFT: Cookbooks.
Classification: LCC TX693 .S63 2018 | DDC 641.82/1--dc23 LC record available at https://lccn.loc.gov/2017042269

Cover design by Jane Sheppard
Cover photograph by Howie Southworth

Print ISBN: 978-1-5107-2814-1
Ebook ISBN: 978-1-5107-2816-5

Printed in China

CONTENTS

INTRODUCTION

Tuna noodle, broccoli cheese, and green bean? Sure, these casseroles are potluck stalwarts. They have a rich history, and may even be made palatable with some kitchen magic. But, let's admit it. As they stand on the back of a cream-of-something soup can, they're played out, tired, and just plain *boring*. To all of you who adore the standard and classic but tasteless, please kiss my . . . *casserole*!

The world is increasingly small. We have unprecedented access to more ingredients, more methods, and more culinary styles than ever before. Fusion, cross-border, hybrid, authentic, throwback, international—whatever you want to call the kitchen personalities we have today, there is no denying that we want to try the untried and reinvent the standard playlist. Today's cooks demand vibrant colors and varied textures to paint their next dinner party. They want to satisfy the family and wow the crowd with a conversation-starting menu. If this is you, *Kiss My Casserole* has your back.

In this book, we dare to update the classics in some surprising ways, and to transport the humble casserole around the globe with delicious, simple, and innovative results. Accessible ingredients and familiar techniques with a touch of the exotic will make you a star on any weeknight, and at the next block party or office luncheon. Your family, neighbors, and colleagues will clamor for more! They should buy this book, too.

In *Kiss My Casserole*, we play all the hits and throw in some dishes you may not even have imagined. We figure, why not look around the world to find inspiration? Ever try a Chinese *shaguo*? How about an Ethiopian *wat*? What? I'll bet you never even thought of cooking up a Icelandic *Ofnsteiktur fiskur með lauk og osti!* Now's your chance! *Kiss My Casserole* is your go-to resource for a new take on the everyday. But first, let's clear up a central issue . . .

WHAT IS A CASSEROLE?

Alton Brown, American television personality, heralded for his scientific approach to cooking, once posited that a casserole was made up of this formula:

1–2 Main Ingredients + Starch + Aromatics + Seasoning + Binder

Now, we understand that his formula often works. But, we ask you, isn't a bit too narrow? What about the Creole cassoulet (page 44)? Definitely a casserole, but without a binder. How about the Indian korma (page 243)? Surely a casserole, but up to a dozen main ingredients. Our Korean jjigae (page 232)? Absolutely a casserole, but with no starch! Indeed, the definition must be broadened.

The word "casserole" itself stems from the French, "casse," or "pan" in English. But, that is way too general and frankly applies to nearly anything that we prepare in the kitchen. Rather than pigeonhole an entire school of cookery into a simple formula or leave it as generically pan-based, we ask several questions about a dish in order to determine whether it should be in this book:

- Is it a jumble of things?
- Does its final texture lie somewhere between a stew and a cake?
- Does it spend time in the oven?
- Does it undergo some physical transformation in there?
- Can you scoop it, or cut it into blocks and/or wedges?
- Don't you just want to cuddle with it?

If the answer to these questions is yes, then it is, indeed, a casserole. It might come to life in a variety of different vessels, shapes, and sizes. It may start on the stovetop and finish under the broiler. It might even be served chilled! Open your mind to casserole diversity. And, if you choose to cuddle your casserole, just be careful.

HOW TO USE THIS BOOK

At the top of every recipe is a handy guide to the essential elements: the total time it will take, what character the dish plays at the meal, suggested cooking vessel, and, last but not least, how many people it is designed to serve. This list of elements is intended to be used while you are scouting for things to try or dishes to compile into a feast. In order to properly balance your time and equipment, as well as choose a main dish, plus accompanying sides, you may dog-ear several pages based upon this critical data.

Total Time

We took the guess work out of how long things take to prep and cook from the word *Go* until *Eat Time*. If a recipe calls for an overnight refrigeration, *BAM!* It's noted right there at the top of the page. If you've got a dinner party at 6:00 p.m. and what you might think was an afternoon off, *WHAMMO!* We warn you that the ratatouille (page 214) takes 3+ hours from the get-go. If a recipe calls for a Total Time of 45 minutes, *YOU'RE WELCOME!* Weeknight dinner is served. But, be forewarned: Casseroles are largely acts of love. Much of this book serves as an ode to the lazy Sunday afternoon.

Character

As with an ensemble cast of a theatrical play, each character at a meal has an important role. Perhaps there is a larger cast of dishes driven by the *Main* as the head-strong lead. Or, maybe those supporting players the *Sides* are the most memorable, adorable parts of the show. If you put together a meal entirely from this book, we promise that every role in the play will shine brightly.

From time to time you run into a dish that is multitalented and can play several roles at different meals. It may be a *Main* for a weeknight, or a *Side* on Thanksgiving, eh? And hey, you may find the most spectacularly gifted dish ever that can perform a *One Pot Meal*, *Main,* and *Side!* It happens.

We also suggest, though it may be obvious, that certain dishes are great for *Breakfast* or *Brunch*. But, don't let us stop you from having breakfast for brunch, lunch, or dinner. We do it, too! It must be said, however, that dinner for breakfast is just weird. Unless it's pizza. Did I mention that we include a *Dessert* chapter just in case you have an empty baking dish hanging around while you're waiting for the Uzbek Plov (page 248) to be done?

Vessels

As noted in the *Introduction*, casseroles come in various shapes, languages, sizes, and yes, cooking vessels. Since we are determined to outlaw the term *casserole dish* as the vehicle in which you create the final dish (a casserole!), our default vessel in *Kiss My Casserole* is the humble 2-inch deep baking dish.

Your baking dish of choice may be that indestructible, square, glass behemoth your grandmother gave you when you moved away to school, or one of the many rainbow of ceramic French beauties now on the market. These days, the choice is also as likely to be a cast iron skillet, a Moroccan tagine, a Chinese clay pot, a Dutch oven, or another straight-sided pan.

Within our *Vessel* suggestion, we note the ideal size for the dish in question. Say, a *9 x 13 inch baking dish, or equivalent*. By equivalent, we mean something that is close to or equal in area to the initially suggested vessel. You can imagine the mess if you try to fit the contents of a suggested 8 x 8 recipe into a 5-inch cake pan, and so on.

The key to figuring out which of your cooking vessels fits the definition of *equivalent* is calculating the surface area of the suggested baking dish. What's the area of your baking dish? Tsk, tsk—your fourth-grade teacher would be disappointed. These equations are important:

Rectangular Vessel Surface Area = Length x Width

Example: 9 x 13 inch lasagna pan = 117 square inches

Example: 8 x 8 inch cake pan = 64 square inches

Circular Vessel Surface Area = 3.14 x Radius^2

Example: 8 inch diameter skillet - 3.14 x 4 inches^2 = 3.14 x 16 = 50 square inches

Example: 10 inch diameter pie pan - 3.14 x 5 inches^2 = 3.14 x 25 = 78½ square inches

So, what do we recommend if the dish you have available doesn't fit our suggestion? It's not complicated—just make more or less. None of our recipes will suffer from doubling, halving, or even three-quartering. For more information, see the *Serving Sizes* section below.

Finally, we assume you know this, but we'll write it out to remind ourselves as well: If a recipe calls for a cast iron skillet as the vessel, we always call for an equivalent oven-safe skillet and not a baking dish, as many of these recipes tend to be dishes that start on the stove and go directly into the oven. *You do not want to use a baking dish on the stovetop.* Yes, we just wrote that in a cookbook.

Serving Sizes

When we suggest that a dish will feed X-Y people, we are not talking about X-Y light-eaters. We're also not talking about heavy-eaters. We're talking about the average eater. If, for example, you have a group of marathon runners coming over for a pasta dinner before the big race tomorrow, *assume "4–6" will serve 2–3!* If you are going to a potluck where folks will be pecking at 16 different casseroles offered by the entire office building, *assume "6–8" will serve 12–16!* If you're throwing a birthday party for a bunch of toddlers . . . Oh, you get the picture.

On doubling or halving recipes, go ahead. Do the simple arithmetic and just remember to choose the right vessel for the job. The cooking times will be roughly accurate, but larger quantities will generally take a bit longer and smaller amounts will be done a bit quicker. We do our best to give you clues on what to look for—like a golden-browned top, slightly jiggly center, crispy cheese, etc. Use those more than the strict timings.

The best advice we can give would be: If you want to double the recipe, just use two of the suggested vessels, or similar. To halve, use a smaller vessel. But we know that this isn't always possible, so don't sweat it if you need to improvise a bit. One of the beauties of casseroles is that they mostly just work. Do be careful, however, when you get to dessert. Baking is more accurately known as chemistry. So, adjustments to amounts must be precise and formulaic. Therefore, we can only recommend doubling a recipe by using two exact vessels of the suggested size.

Special Diets, Substitutions, etc.

If a recipe is already in line with a specialized diet, it is indicated below the name of the dish.

You will find recipes that are natively *Vegetarian*, *Vegan*, and *Gluten-Free*.

Though this book is not designed for a specialized audience, we do find it important for you to know (going into a cooking adventure) that you do not have to think about adapting our brilliant ideas to fit your lifestyle.

But, in the remote case where our idea of brilliance doesn't align precisely with yours, feel free to leave out an undesired ingredient, just don't leave out any star of the show. *Green Grains Casserole* (page 40) without the barley is just a delicious green puddle. Other than that, here are four of our favorite substitutions:

Flour (as a thickener or coating)—Use rice flour or potato starch. We find that when you're making a béchamel (white sauce), dusting meat, or sprinkling flour over sautéing vegetables in order to thicken the impending sauce, these two do an excellent job, and in some cases, make for smoother, silkier product. By the way, rice flour is used for tempura. Tempura's delicious. Okay, back to casseroles.

Mammalian Meat—If this substitution applies to you, you've already shopped the heck out of meat stand-ins. You already know your way around not-dogs and faux-sage. From where we sit, it may be enough to simply replace meat with fake meat for the sake of simplicity. But we really like products that add their own character to a dish. For example, have you tried baked tofu? Tempeh? Wheat gluten? Trust us.

Pasta—This is a tough nut to crack. The problem is that most gluten-free pastas in the market have a tendency to get overly mushy during normal cook-times. Can you imagine what will happen to them when they then bake *in a casserole for an hour*? In our experience, there are no perfect options, but corn or corn + quinoa pastas are probably the best options.

Chile Spices—There are many dishes in this book that include chile powders, fresh chile peppers, as well as dried chiles. They add a zesty character to a dish, but this is an easy one to replace. If you are not a spice-lover, you could simply skip it, sub out a hot chile powder with mild, or swap fresh chiles for bell peppers. In our experience, a given dish will shine on another level with these replacements made. You're not alone. You deserve great food!

Global Recipes

The majority of *Kiss My Casserole* spends its time outside of the Americas, spanning the globe. We include dishes as common as English shepherd's pie (though sheepless), (page 155), and as outlandish as Japanese doria (page 218). We've tried hard to keep the flavors of our international casseroles authentic, though in some cases we take creative license with the format to make it easier to prepare as a casserole.

For example, there's a famous dish in Shanghai called *Lion's Head Meatballs* (page 228). Not surprisingly, the original dish is a few huge meatballs. But, in order to keep the balance of meat to cabbage and noodles, we adapt the meatballs into layers using the same ingredients. We retain the core textures and flavors of the dish by altering the format a tad.

Across all our global recipes, we sought to keep the ingredients accessible to the average consumer, or at the very least we suggest alternative/replacement ingredients that approximate the original or native ingredient used in the home country. We think we did a bang-up job, and in some cases, dare we say, improved upon the original? Enjoy *Kiss My Casserole* and let us know how we've done!

The Americas

Biscuits and Red Gravy Casserole

USA

TOTAL TIME: 1 hour
CHARACTER: Breakfast, Main
VESSEL: 9 x 13 inch baking dish, or equivalent
SERVES: 6–8

My home in Alexandria, Virginia is the culinary Mason-Dixon line. Or, as I call it, the Hash-Biscuits line. You see, when I travel North, I assess the fitness of a classic diner by its corned beef hash. But, when I drive south, my eyes shift to the biscuits and gravy! The deeper I go, the spicier I expect it to be. Here lies my ode to what biscuits and gravy should be right around, say, Atlanta. Oh, and out of fairness, anything spicy should be red in hue. Pro tip.

—Howie

GRAVY:

¼ cup extra-virgin olive oil
¼ cup + 1 Tbsp unsalted butter, divided
1 lb Andouille or other smoked sausage, finely diced
3 Tbsp tomato paste
½ cup all-purpose flour
5 cups milk
1 Tbsp hot paprika
1 tsp salt
1 cup parsley, chopped, divided

BISCUIT TOPPING:

3 cups all-purpose flour
4 tsp baking powder
1 tsp baking soda
1½ Tbsp sugar
1 tsp salt
¾ cup unsalted butter, cold, ¼ inch cubes
1¼ cup buttermilk
2 Tbsp extra-virgin olive oil

Preheat oven to 400°F. To make the gravy, heat olive oil and ¼ cup of the butter in a skillet over medium heat. Once the butter melts, add sausage into the skillet. Sauté the sausage until lightly browned, about 3 minutes. Stir in tomato paste. Sprinkle flour into the skillet and sauté this mixture for 2 minutes, stirring regularly. Slowly whisk in the milk, making sure there are no lumps. Stir in paprika, salt, and ½ cup of parsley. Continue to stir the mixture until it comes to a boil.

continued on page 12

Reduce the heat to low and allow the gravy to simmer, stirring occasionally, until it reaches a creamy gravy consistency, about 6 minutes. Using the remaining 1 tablespoon of butter, grease the bottom and sides of a baking dish. Carefully transfer skillet contents to the baking dish.

To make the biscuits, in a large mixing bowl, whisk together the flour, baking soda, baking powder, sugar, and salt. Add the butter cubes and incorporate into the flour mixture with a pastry cutter or squeeze with your fingertips until all pieces of butter are consistently smaller than peas. Add the buttermilk and quickly mix well with your hands, until dough forms.

Dust the counter or a board with flour and transfer your dough from the bowl. Dust the top of the dough with more flour and begin to flatten and mold with your hand or a floured rolling pin. Roll the dough until it is a ¾-inch thick rectangle. Fold the dough in half once and roll back to ¾ inch thick. Cut the dough into rough squares. Place dough squares atop the gravy in the baking dish. It's okay if they sink into the gravy a bit. You may have extra dough—bake standalone biscuits on an ungreased baking sheet.

Drizzle the top of the dough squares with 2 tablespoons of olive oil. Transfer the baking dish to the oven and bake for 25–30 minutes, or until the biscuit tops are golden brown. Allow the casserole to cool for 5 minutes and garnish with the remaining parsley before scooping out some of the gravy with each biscuit.

Berry Blintz Casserole

USA

TOTAL TIME: 1 hour, 30 minutes
CHARACTER: Breakfast, Main, Dessert
VESSEL: 9 x 13 inch baking dish, or equivalent
SERVES: 4–6

> Blintzes are great. But I like to sleep late. So, if I'm hosting brunch, there's no way that I'm waking up early enough to prepare 20 perfect little crepes, neatly stuffed and perfectly folded. This is the lazy-person's version—10% of the work, 100% of the taste. And, you can always go back to bed while it's in the oven!
>
> —Greg

FILLING:

1½ lb ricotta cheese (about 3 cups)
1 lb cream cheese
2 eggs, beaten
¼ cup sugar
¼ cup lemon juice (about 1 large lemon)
1 tsp lemon zest, grated
1 tsp orange zest, grated
¼ tsp salt

BLINTZ BATTER:

1 cup flour
½ cup sugar
1 Tbsp baking powder
¼ tsp salt
3 eggs, beaten
¼ cup whole milk
1 tsp vanilla extract
1 cup + 1 tsp butter, melted

SAUCE:

½ cup apple juice
¼ cup sugar
6 cups frozen or fresh berries (about 1½ pounds)
2 Tbsp cornstarch
2 Tbsp water

Preheat oven to 300°F.

To make the filling, combine all ingredients in a bowl or stand mixer. Stir to combine fully.

To make the batter, in a large mixing bowl, whisk together flour, sugar, baking powder, and salt. In another mixing bowl, beat the eggs, milk, and vanilla together until well combined. Pour the wet ingredients into the dry, add 1 cup of melted butter, and whisk until smooth.

continued on page 15

Prepare the baking dish by coating it with the remaining teaspoon of melted butter. To assemble, pour in half of the blintz batter, making a very thin layer. Then gently pour the filling, being sure to pour it in the center and around the outsides, to give an even coat. Use a rubber spatula to even the top of the filling, and layer the remaining blintz batter on top. Bake at 300°F for 75 minutes, or until the top crust is golden brown, and casserole jiggles slightly.

While the dish is baking, prepare the sauce. Place a pot over medium heat. Pour in the apple juice and the sugar. Stir until sugar is completely dissolved. Add the berries and cook for 5–10 minutes, or until the berries have mostly broken down. In a small bowl, create a slurry by combining the cornstarch and water. Slowly stir slurry into the pot to thicken the sauce.

Remove blintz casserole from the oven and allow to cool at least 15 minutes. Serve with drizzled sauce and additional fresh fruit for a lovely brunch or dessert.

NY Bagel and Lox Casserole

USA

TOTAL TIME: 20 minutes, plus overnight, plus 1 hour, 15 minutes
CHARACTER: Breakfast, Main
VESSEL: 9 x 13 inch baking dish, or equivalent
SERVES: 6–8

3 large bagels (about 1 lb), cut into 1-inch pieces
½ small red onion, diced
8 oz cherry tomatoes, halved
2 scallions, sliced thinly
7 eggs
2 cups half-and-half or milk
1 tsp salt
1 tsp garlic powder
3 Tbsp extra-virgin olive oil, divided
8 oz cream cheese, cubed
8 oz Nova lox or smoked salmon, diced

Facial hair can be awesome. I love my effortless ability to grow on-demand face art. I've gone through thousands of permutations in my life: full-on caveman, Civil War mustachioed sideburns, mutton chops, soul goatee, and the list goes on. Over the years, to my great chagrin, I have found that attempting to gracefully eat an open-faced bagel while wearing such an ostentatious beard is a near impossibility. Whiskers and cream cheese are natural enemies. So, what's a bearded guy to do? Casserole it.

—Howie

In a large mixing bowl, toss the bagel pieces with red onion, cherry tomatoes, and scallions until well mixed. In another mixing bowl, whisk together eggs, half-and-half or milk, salt, and garlic powder.

Coat the bottom and sides of a baking dish with 1 tablespoon of the olive oil. Evenly distribute half of the bagel mixture in the baking dish. Dot the mixture with cream cheese cubes and salmon. Layer the remaining bread mixture atop the cream cheese and salmon. Be sure to keep it as even as possible (no bagel hills).

Slowly pour the egg mixture evenly over the bagel mixture, being sure that some of the liquid reaches most, if not all, of the bread. Use the back of a wooden spoon, a clean hand, or spatula, to compress the whole mixture to ensure that the liquid is evenly distributed.

Cover the baking dish with plastic wrap and refrigerate overnight.

Preheat the oven to 375°F. Remove the baking dish from the refrigerator, discard the plastic wrap, and cover tightly with aluminum foil. Transfer the baking dish to the center rack of the oven. Bake for 35 minutes. Remove the baking dish from the oven, and drizzle the top with the remaining 2 tablespoons of olive oil. Transfer the baking dish back into the oven and bake for an additional 35–40 minutes, or until the top is golden brown and crusty.

Remove the casserole from the oven and allow it to cool for 15 minutes before slicing and serving.

French Toast Bake

USA

TOTAL TIME: 2 hours
CHARACTER: Breakfast, Main
VESSEL: 9 x 13 inch baking dish, or equivalent
SERVES: 6–8

5 eggs
2 cups half-and-half or milk
3 Tbsp sugar
1 tsp cinnamon
1 tsp salt
1 tsp vanilla extract
1 Tbsp butter
1 cup pure maple syrup or pancake syrup, divided, plus more for drizzling
5 cups (about 1 lb) crusty bread cut into 1-inch pieces
Whipped cream, berries, and additional syrup for serving

> In our previous book, *One Pan to Rule Them All*, I joked about my childhood obsession with what a French toaster must look like. I'll let that sink in for a moment . . . okay, onto the matter at hand. Delicately crispy, decadently unctuous, sweet, buttery, sinfully delicious. French toast, when expertly made, is outstanding. When made for a crowd, it can be a disaster. Splatters of blackened butter Jackson Pollocked across the kitchen wall, near-burned crust surrounding an eggy substance previously known as bread. Stop it. This casserole saves lives.
>
> —Greg

In a large mixing bowl, whisk together eggs, half-and-half or milk, sugar, cinnamon, salt, and vanilla. Smear butter across the bottom and sides of a baking dish. Pour ½ cup of the syrup in the baking dish. Evenly add bread pieces—be sure you have one even layer with a flat top (no bread hills).

Slowly pour the egg mixture evenly over the bread mixture, being sure that some of the liquid reaches most, if not all, of the bread. Use the back of a wooden spoon, a clean hand, or spatula, to compress the whole mixture to ensure that the liquid is evenly distributed. Cover with plastic wrap and set aside for at least 1 hour (or in the refrigerator overnight).

Preheat the oven to 375°F. Remove plastic wrap and drizzle the remaining syrup evenly across the top of the mixture. Bake for 30–35 minutes on the center rack of the oven, or until the top is beginning to brown and get crusty.

Remove the casserole from the oven, scoop hot servings with an oversized spoon! Dress with whipped cream, berries, and/or maple syrup and enjoy!

Tex-Mex Egg Puff

USA

TOTAL TIME: 1 hour, 35 minutes
CHARACTER: Breakfast, Main
VESSEL: 8 x 8 inch baking dish, or equivalent
SERVES: 4–6

1 sheet frozen puff pastry
Flour for dusting
1 15-oz can black beans, drained
1 4-oz can Hatch or other green chiles (hot or mild), diced
2 cups Monterey or Colby Jack cheese, shredded, divided
3 scallions, thinly sliced
6 large eggs
1 cup half-and-half or cream
½ tsp salt
½ tsp ground black pepper
2 small or 1 large corn or wheat tortillas, cut into 1-inch pieces
Sour cream for serving

When I was in high school, my buddies and I would occasionally get together to experience something new and exotic at a "Mexican" joint that popped up. Encheritos! In South Jersey! The 1980s were weird. Then, I moved to California for college. Ohhh, if *this* is Mexican food then *that* was . . . what, exactly? That's when I came to appreciate the cuisine of the Texas-Mexico borderlands.

—Howie

Remove puff pastry sheet from the freezer and allow to thaw, within its parchment on the counter, for about 30 minutes.

Preheat the oven to 425°F. Dust your counter or board with flour, unfold the puff pastry and place the sheet atop the flour, and dust with some more flour. Roll the sheet into a 10-inch square, smoothing out all the fold seams.

Transfer the pastry to a baking dish, letting it settle into the bottom and along the sides. (This may take some manual encouragement.) Trim the edges back to the rim of the baking dish, but make sure the pastry covers the vessel like a pie crust.

Place the beans in the pastry in one layer. Next, scatter the chiles atop the beans, then 1 cup of the cheese in a single layer and top with the scallions. In a large mixing bowl, whisk together the eggs, cream, salt, and pepper. Carefully, pour the mixture into the pastry shell, trying not to disturb the contents. The scallions may wish to float, and that's okay. Be who you want to be, you know what I mean?

Cover the surface of the egg mixture with pieces of tortilla, forming a blanket. Sprinkle the remaining 1 cup of cheese on top. Bake in the oven for 30–35 minutes, or until the center is no longer jiggly and the cheese is golden brown.

Remove the egg puff from the oven and allow it to cool on the counter for at least 20 minutes. Cut into 4–6 slices. It can be served warm, but it's better at room temperature with a dollop of sour cream.

All American Breakfast Casserole

USA

TOTAL TIME: 1 hour
CHARACTER: Breakfast, Main
VESSEL: 8 x 8 inch baking dish, or equivalent
SERVES: 4–6

1 Tbsp extra-virgin olive oil
3 cups frozen hash browns
6 slices bacon, diced
8 eggs, beaten
½ cup half-and-half
½ tsp salt
¼ tsp ground black pepper
¼ tsp cayenne pepper (optional)
2 cups sharp cheddar cheese, shredded

As a child, my dear Uncle Jon absolutely insisted that his food not intermingle. Spaghetti was not to meet meatball. Peanut butter was to have at least a half-inch buffer from jelly. He would not have been a fan of this dish, which takes all the best parts of breakfast and bakes them into one gooey, smoky, delicious bite. Sorry, Uncle Jon. I'll make you a deconstructed version next time!

—Greg

Preheat the oven to 400°F.

Coat the inside of a baking dish with the olive oil. Place the hash browns along the bottom of the dish. Lay out the bacon on top of the hash browns, in as much of a single layer as possible—a bit of overlapping is fine. Transfer the baking dish to the oven and roast for 25 minutes, or until bacon is browned and crispy.

While the bacon and potatoes are cooking, whisk the eggs, half-and-half, salt, pepper and, if you are using it, cayenne, until well combined and frothy. Add the cheese and whisk until combined.

Lower the oven to 350°F. Remove a few pieces of cooked bacon from the dish for topping and carefully redistribute the remaining bacon to evenly cover the potatoes. Give the cheese and eggs a good stir, and pour into the baking dish. Top with the reserved bacon and place back in the oven. Cook for 25–30 minutes, or until the eggs and cheese have browned.

Serve hot blocks with salsa, or a dash of hot sauce.

Feta Leek Breakfast Bake

USA

TOTAL TIME: 1 hour, 20 minutes
CHARACTER: Breakfast, Main
VESSEL: 8 x 8 inch baking dish, or equivalent
SERVES: 4–6

> Passover is a full week where we Jews go Paleo. No bread. No oats. Not even spelt! Well, every year, my family looks forward to this week, largely because it gives us the excuse to make rich, custardy, breakfasts like this one. Don't worry, I'll be eating it next April. But I give you permission to eat it tomorrow!
>
> —Greg

¼ cup + 1 Tbsp butter, divided
1 large leek, thinly sliced into rings
½ tsp salt
1 cup heavy cream
5 eggs, beaten
1 cup feta cheese, crumbled
½ tsp black pepper
¼ tsp nutmeg

Preheat the oven to 350°F.

Add ¼ cup of butter to a skillet and place over medium heat. When the butter is melted, and beginning to bubble, add the leek and salt. Sauté until the leek is cooked through and limp, about 15 minutes.

While the leek is cooking, in a mixing bowl combine the cream, eggs, cheese, pepper, and nutmeg. When the leeks are cooked, add them to the bowl and stir to combine.

Prepare the baking dish by coating it in 1 tablespoon of butter. Pour the egg, cheese, and leek mixture into the dish, and bake for one hour, or until the casserole is set and the top is golden brown. Remove the breakfast bake from the oven and serve in wonderfully aromatic scoops.

Broccoli Cheese Casserole 2.0

USA

TOTAL TIME: 1 hour, 20 minutes
CHARACTER: Side
VESSEL: 8 x 8 inch baking dish, or equivalent
SERVES: 6–8

2 Tbsp extra-virgin olive oil
1 large onion, thinly sliced
2 sheets puff pastry, frozen
2 cups broccoli florets
Flour for dusting
1 lb brie cheese (1 whole wheel or wedges)
1 egg, beaten

> Dear Broccoli Cheese Casserole: There comes a time in the life of every recipe when it needs its head examined. We feel it's high time that you fess up to your reliance on canned cream of mushroom soup! Fly, be free of interloper ingredients who try to sully your good name! Except for caramelized onions. There's always room for caramelized onions. Here, we give you your identity back. Rock on, you casserole, you. Also, you look a lot like your cousin, brie en croute!
>
> —Greg

Preheat the oven to 400°F.

Place a skillet over medium heat and add the oil. When the oil begins to shimmer, add the onion. Sauté until the onions begin to turn translucent, about 6–8 minutes. Reduce the heat to medium-low and continue to stir the onions for 30–35 minutes. They will become very soft and very brown. This is what you want. When done, remove the onions to a plate.

While the onions are caramelizing, remove puff pastry sheets from the freezer and allow to thaw, folded on the counter, for about 30 minutes. Also, while the onions are taking their sweet time (see what I did there?), in a separate pot, boil or steam the broccoli florets for 3–4 minutes. When the broccoli is done, drain and remove it to a plate to cool a while we await the completion of the caramelized onions.

Dust your counter or board with flour, unfold the puff pastry sheets and place them atop the flour, and dust with some more flour. Pinch the edges of the two pastry sheets together to form one rectangle of pastry. Using a rolling pin, roll the joined sheet to 20 x 10 inches, smoothing out all the fold seams.

continued on page 28

Transfer the pastry to a baking dish, letting it settle into the bottom and along the sides. (This may take some manual encouragement.) The sheet should hang from two opposite sides by several inches.

Cut the brie wheel or wedges in half, like a sandwich roll. Place half of the brie in top of the pastry at the bottom of the baking dish. Top the cheese with the broccoli, followed by the caramelized onions. Place the remaining half of brie atop the onions. You've basically made a broccoli and onion sandwich with brie for bread – resist the urge to take a bite.

Cover the brie by folding the loose, overhanging ends of the pastry over the top. Tuck any extra pastry into the sides of the baking dish. Brush the top of the pastry with beaten egg. Transfer the baking dish to the oven and bake for 30–35 minutes or until the pastry is golden brown.

Allow the casserole to cool for 10 minutes before you dig in and let the oozy cheese, broccoli, and onions free of their buttery cage!

Tuna Casserole 2.0

USA

TOTAL TIME: 1 hour, 10 minutes
CHARACTER: One Pot Meal, Main, Side
VESSEL: 9 x 13 inch baking dish, or equivalent
SERVES: 6–8

For years now, my beautiful wife Jessica has claimed to hate *hot tuna*. Naturally, I've been known to poke fun at this. When developing this book, we knew that tuna casserole not only had to be subject to the spotlight, but take on a new, modern incarnation. But, I vowed to keep it hot and win her over to the dark side! Flash forward to today, just now, outside on the sidewalk. A very good friend told me that he and his kin also *hate* hot tuna. What? This is a *thing*? Here I thought this recipe was meant to sway merely one dubious soul. Now, I am convinced that the world needs this recipe. Long live hot tuna.

—Howie

3 qt water
1 large head cauliflower, florets
¼ cup (½ stick) butter
¼ cup flour
2 cups milk
1 tsp salt
1 tsp ground black pepper
1 tsp smoked paprika
1½ cups Monterey Jack cheese, shredded
½ cup mayonnaise
1 egg
2 stalks celery, thinly sliced
2 5-oz cans tuna in water, drained, flaked
2 Tbsp extra-virgin olive oil, divided
1 cup Japanese panko or other bread crumbs
¾ cup Parmesan cheese, grated

Preheat the oven to 375°F.

In a large pot, bring water to a boil over high heat. Boil the cauliflower florets for 3–4 minutes. Drain and remove the florets to a plate to cool a while you prepare the remainder of the ingredients.

Place a skillet over medium heat and add butter. When the butter melts, sprinkle in the flour and whisk to combine completely. Continue to whisk the mixture for 2 minutes. Slowly pour in the milk while continuing to whisk briskly, to ensure the sauce is smooth with no lumps. Stir in salt, pepper. and paprika. Reduce the heat to low and let the mixture simmer, stirring occasionally for 8 minutes. Remove the mixture to a large mixing bowl, stir in the cheese, and allow to cool for at least 10 minutes.

continued on page 31

Once the milk and cheese mixture has cooled, stir in the mayonnaise and egg. Mix thoroughly. Fold in the cauliflower, celery, and tuna. Coat the bottom and sides of a baking dish with 1 tablespoon of olive oil. Pour the contents of the mixing bowl into the baking dish.

In a second mixing bowl, combine the bread crumbs, Parmesan cheese, and the remaining 1 tablespoon of olive oil. As evenly as possible, coat the top of the cauliflower mixture with the bread crumb mixture. Transfer the baking dish to the oven and bake for 40–45 minutes or until the top is golden and crusty.

Serve hot scoops directly to hungry bowls.

Green Bean Casserole 2.0

USA

TOTAL TIME: 1 hour, 10 minutes
CHARACTER: Side
VESSEL: 9 x 13 inch baking dish, or equivalent
SERVES: 6–8

I'm not sure how it happened, but it seems that mid-20th-century American cuisine became afraid of extreme heat. Perhaps they had inferior potholders? Or maybe something to do with the Cold War? I'm not sure, but I do know that the rediscovery of the high-heat roast can breathe new life into the tired, overcooked family classics. I humbly present to you our well-needed, *roasted* green bean update.

—Greg

1½ lb fresh green beans, trimmed, snapped into halves
2 Tbsp extra-virgin olive oil, divided
¾ tsp salt, divided
¼ tsp ground black pepper
6 slices bacon, diced
1 large onion, diced
1 cup mushrooms, thinly sliced
3 cloves garlic, minced
2 Tbsp flour
½ cup chicken broth or water
1 cup cream
1 cup canned French fried onions (optional)

Preheat the oven to 425°F.

In a large mixing bowl, add green beans, 1½ tablespoons of olive oil, ½ teaspoon of salt, and pepper. Toss until beans are evenly coated. Spread out along the bottom of a baking dish, and place in the oven for 25–30 minutes, tossing halfway through the cooking. Remove when they are beginning to wrinkle and brown.

While the beans are roasting, add the remaining ½ tablespoon of olive oil into a skillet. Place the skillet over medium-high heat. When the oil shimmers, add the bacon and sauté until it begins to brown, about 4–6 minutes. Add the onion and the mushrooms, and continue to sauté until the onions are limp, about another 4–6 minutes. Add the garlic and sauté until fragrant, about 30 seconds. Sprinkle flour over the skillet mixture and continue to sauté until the flour is completely incorporated. Add the broth (or water), cream, and the remaining ¼ tsp of salt. Reduce the heat to medium-low and scrape the bottom of the skillet to bring up the brown bits. Simmer until the sauce begins to thicken, about 2–4 minutes.

When the green beans are roasted, they should look slightly brown and wrinkly. Remove them from the oven, and pour the bacon cream sauce over them. If you are going for the 1950s fun, layer on the French fried onions. Lower the oven to 350°F and return the baking dish to the oven for 10–15 minutes, or until the cream sauce is further thickened, bubbly, and the optional fried onion topping begins to crisp.

Serve with roasted chicken, roasted turkey, or another roasted slab of your choice.

Chicken Pot Pie 2.0

USA

TOTAL TIME: 2 hours
CHARACTER: One Pot Meal, Main
VESSEL: 8 x 8 inch baking dish, 4–6 ramekins, or equivalent
SERVES: 4–6

Growing up in Los Angeles, it would have been hard to avoid developing a strong affinity for Mexican food. But it's unclear why anyone would ever *want* to avoid such a wonderful, wonderful affinity! This chile verde-inspired casserole has all the classic pot pie ingredients—chicken, carrots, peas, and potatoes. But it's the jalapeños, tomatillos, and cilantro that make it amazing.

—Greg

- 1 sheet frozen pie dough
- 10 tomatillos, husked and diced
- 2 jalapeño peppers, stemmed, optionally seeded
- 6 cloves garlic
- 1 cup cilantro, roughly chopped
- 1½ tsp sugar
- 2 tsp salt, divided
- 1½ cups, plus 1 Tbsp water, divided
- 3 Tbsp all-purpose flour
- ¼ tsp black pepper
- 1½ lb chicken thighs, boneless, skinless, diced
- 2 Tbsp vegetable oil
- 1 large onion, diced
- 1 Tbsp ground cumin
- 2 tsp dried oregano
- 1 (about 1 cup) carrot, diced
- 1 (about ½ lb) russet potato, peeled, diced
- ½ cup frozen peas
- 1 egg

Thaw the frozen pie dough, as directed by the package.

Add tomatillos, jalapeños, garlic, cilantro, sugar, 1 teaspoon of the salt, and 1½ cups of water to a blender. Blend until smooth.

In a small mixing bowl, combine the flour, the remaining 1 teaspoon of salt, and the pepper. Dip the chicken into the seasoned flour, turning to coat. Shake off excess and reserve on a plate.

continued on page 36

Heat oil in a skillet over medium-high heat. When the oil begins to shimmer, add half of the chicken, and sauté until browned, about 5–6 minutes. Using a slotted spoon, remove the browned chicken to a plate. Repeat with the remaining chicken, reserving it to the same plate when browned.

Into the hot, empty skillet, add the onion and sauté until almost translucent, about 4–6 minutes. Add the cumin and oregano, continuing to sauté until fragrant, about 30 seconds. Add the green sauce from your blender, and using a spatula, free the browned bits from the bottom of the skillet. Bring the sauce to a boil, and lower the heat to a simmer. Add the browned chicken, along with the carrot and potato, and allow to simmer, uncovered, for 15 minutes. Remove from heat, add the frozen peas, and allow the stew to cool for at least 30 minutes.

Preheat the oven to 350°F.

Transfer the contents of the skillet to either a single baking dish or ramekins. Cover the baking dish(es) with thawed pie crust. Pinch the crust to seal the edges, cutting off any excess crust. Make a few slits along the top to allow steam to escape the pie. Beat the egg and remaining 1 tablespoon of water together. Using a pastry brush, paint the top of the dough with this egg wash.

Transfer the baking dish(es) to the oven and bake for 45–50 minutes, or until the crust has browned. Remove the pot pie(s) from the oven and allow them to rest for 10 minutes before serving.

Cajun Okra and Tomato Bake

USA

TOTAL TIME: 50 minutes then overnight, plus 1 hour, 15 minutes
CHARACTER: Side
VESSEL: 9 x 13 inch baking dish, or equivalent
SERVES: 8-10

People have a problem with okra, and I *get* it. It can be downright slimy when not cooked right. *Hey, what's this new Cajun dish you're feeding me?* Two bites in: *Eeew, Cajun's ruined forever!* That goop is called mucilage, a by-product of natural sugars that break down as the okra fruit—yes, fruit—ripens. The acids in a tomato break down this offensive mess, so the two are a match made in heaven. And . . . with Cajun potentially *ruined forever*, here we solve that problem!

—Howie

CORNBREAD:

3 cups yellow cornmeal
1 tsp salt
1 tsp baking soda
2 Tbsp baking powder
1 Tbsp sugar
2½ cups buttermilk
¾ cup + 1 Tbsp extra-virgin olive oil, divided
3 eggs

THE BAKE:

2 Tbsp extra-virgin olive oil, divided
1 large onion, diced
2 tsp salt, divided
1 clove garlic, minced
2 tsp dried oregano
1 tsp smoked paprika
1 tsp ground cayenne pepper
1 tsp ground black pepper
12 oz frozen sliced okra, thawed
1 28-oz can diced tomatoes
2 lb prepared cornbread, from above or store-bought
3 large eggs
2 cups vegetable broth or water

continued on page 39

To make the cornbread from scratch, preheat the oven to 375°F. In a large mixing bowl, whisk together the cornmeal, salt, baking soda, baking powder, and sugar. In a separate mixing bowl, whisk together the buttermilk, ¾ cup of the olive oil, and eggs. Stir the wet ingredients into the dry ingredients until combined completely. Do not overmix.

Coat the bottom and sides of a cast iron skillet or baking dish with the remaining 1 tablespoon of olive oil. Scrape the cornbread batter into the vessel and transfer to the oven for 35-40 minutes, or until the top begins to brown and crack.

Remove the cornbread from the oven and set it on a cooling rack on the counter, uncovered, overnight to dry out.

To make the bake, preheat the oven to 375°F. Place a skillet over medium heat and add 1 tablespoon of olive oil. When the oil begins to shimmer, add onion and 1 teaspoon of salt, and sauté until the onion becomes almost translucent, about 6-8 minutes. Add garlic to the skillet and continue to sauté for 1 additional minute. Remove the onion mixture to a large mixing bowl.

To this bowl, mix in the oregano, paprika, cayenne, black pepper, okra, tomatoes, and the remaining 1 teaspoon of salt. Then roughly crumble pre-made cornbread on top.

In a separate bowl, whisk together eggs and broth or water. Pour the egg mixture into the bread mixture. Stir to combine until the liquid is fully absorbed.

Using a paper towel or pastry brush, coat the bottom and sides of a baking dish with the remaining 1 tablespoon of olive oil. Pour the contents of the mixing bowl into a baking dish, gently pressing to ensure everything fits in one solid layer. Place the baking dish onto the center rack of the oven and bake for 45-50 minutes, or until the top is slightly browned and crusty. Allow the bake to rest for 10 minutes before serving heaping spoonfuls.

Green Grains Casserole

USA

TOTAL TIME: 1 hour, 20 minutes
CHARACTER: Side
VESSEL: 8 x 8 inch baking dish, or equivalent
SERVES: 6-8

When I was a kid, I loved watching Popeye. Though it took me years to find an equal love for spinach, I always kept in the back of my mind that this magical green was good for my biceps and that olive oil, er, Olive Oyl was to be cherished at all cost! *Take that, Bluto!* Here, the green machine meets its match, barley. Barley is used to make beer. So, if you think about it, eating this is like sharing a cold one with Popeye. Or, maybe that's just me. It's delicious, and rather healthy.

—Greg

2 cups pearled barley, uncooked
4 cups water, boiling
2½ tsp salt, divided
4 Tbsp extra-virgin olive oil, divided
1 large onion, diced
1½ lb baby spinach
2 cloves garlic, minced
2 jalapeño peppers, stemmed, seeded, minced
1 cup heavy cream
1 tsp ground black pepper
1 cup Parmesan cheese, grated or shredded
2 eggs, beaten
½ cup cilantro, chopped
Sour cream for serving

Preheat the oven to 350°F.

In a baking dish, mix barley, boiling water, 2 teaspoons of salt, and 2 tablespoons extra-virgin olive oil. Cover tightly with aluminum foil and bake for 1 hour. Remove from the oven and coolest aside.

Place a skillet over medium heat and add 1 tablespoon of olive oil. When the oil shimmers, add the onion and sauté until it becomes translucent, about 6-8 minutes. Add the spinach in batches until it all wilts. Add garlic and jalapeño and continue to sauté until most of the liquid has evaporated, about 4-6 additional minutes.

In a blender, combine half of the skillet contents with cream, pepper, cheese, and remaining ½ teaspoon of salt. Purée until smooth. Add the eggs and purée once again. In a large mixing bowl, combine cooked barley, puréed blender mixture, the remainder of the skillet contents and cilantro.

Coat the bottom and sides of a baking dish with the remaining 1 tablespoon of olive oil. Scrape the mixing bowl contents into the baking dish. Cover tightly with aluminum foil and bake in the oven for 30 minutes. Remove the baking dish from the oven and carefully remove the foil. Return to the oven for an additional 10 minutes, or until the top begins to turn brown.

Remove the casserole from the oven and serve hot scoops. You may wish to serve it topped with sour cream!

Jambalaya Z'Herbes

USA

TOTAL TIME: 1 hour, 20 minutes
CHARACTER: One Pot Meal
VESSEL: 12-inch cast iron skillet with a lid, or other oven-safe skillet with a lid
SERVES: 4–6

- 2 Tbsp olive oil
- ½ lb bacon, diced
- ½ lb smoked ham, diced
- 1 small onion, diced
- 1 green bell pepper, diced
- 3 stalks celery, thinly sliced
- 1 tsp ground cayenne pepper or red pepper flakes
- 1 tsp ground cumin
- 1 tsp smoked paprika
- 1 tsp salt
- 1 tsp ground black pepper
- 12 oz spinach, Swiss chard, or other tender green, rinsed, trimmed, roughly chopped
- 1 clove garlic, minced
- 1 tsp dried oregano
- 1 cup cherry tomatoes, halved
- 1¼ cups chicken stock or broth
- 1 cup jasmine or other long grain rice, uncooked

> I spend plenty of time in New Orleans. When I'm there, I'm not *officially* present until I find the nearest bowl of *gumbo z'herbes*, a luscious stew of smoked meat, silky broth, and lovely, tender greens. When I try to serve this style of gumbo at home, I tell my jambalaya-obsessed kids that gumbo is just like jambalaya if you take out the rice and serve it on the side! Well, that didn't fly . . . So, I started making this hybrid, equally delicious version of jambalaya to everyone's content.
>
> —Howie

Preheat your oven to 375°F.

Place a skillet over medium heat and add the olive oil. When the oil begins to shimmer, add the bacon to the skillet and sauté, stirring often, until the edges of the bacon are brown, about 3–4 minutes. Add ham, onion, bell pepper, celery, cayenne, cumin, paprika, salt, pepper, and sauté with the meats until the onion becomes almost translucent, about 6 more minutes. Add the chopped greens and sauté for an additional 4-6 minutes, or until the greens wilt completely.

Add in the garlic and sauté for one more minute. Add oregano, tomatoes, and stock to the skillet and bring to a boil. Pour in the rice and stir to distribute throughout the skillet. Cover and move the skillet to the oven for 30 minutes.

Remove the skillet from the oven. Allow the jambalaya to rest for 15 minutes. Remove the lid and serve directly to bowls.

Creole Cassoulet

USA

TOTAL TIME: 2 hours then overnight, plus 2 hours, 30 minutes
CHARACTER: Main
VESSEL: 9 x 13 inch baking dish, or equivalent
SERVES: 10-12

One brisk winter's night, I happened upon a small country inn whilst seeking the warmth of jovial conversation by the light of a roaring fire. Okay, maybe in my fantasies . . . It was actually on K street in Washington, DC, and I was meeting a friend for a beer at a chic Belgian alehouse. Anyhow, what warmed my chilly urban reality was a satisfying crock of cassoulet, a hearty, earthy, smoky casserole of beans, sausage, and cured poultry. Cassoulet transported me as I dismissed the fact that my buddy was an hour late! Enjoy our version of cassoulet, with a Louisiana twist. The aroma while it bubbles away will guarantee you won't have to enjoy it alone!

—Howie

CONFIT CHICKEN THIGHS:

4 chicken thighs, bone-in, skin on
2 tsp salt
1 tsp ground black pepper
2 garlic cloves halved
2 scallions, cut into 2-inch pieces
1 Tbsp dried oregano
1 cup extra-virgin olive oil

CASSEROLE:

1 large onion, chopped
2 stalks celery, sliced thinly
1 red bell pepper, diced
1 tsp salt
1 tsp ground black pepper
1 tsp smoked paprika
2 cloves garlic, minced
1 cup tomato purée
1 cup chicken stock
3 14½-oz cans red kidney beans, drained and rinsed
1 lb smoked sausage, cut into 3-inch pieces

Preheat the oven to 250°F. To make the confit, place the chicken snugly in the bottom of an oven-safe skillet. Ideally, the skillet is just large enough to fit all of the chicken thighs, without too much extra space. Sprinkle the chicken with salt and pepper, scatter the remaining confit seasonings around the chicken. Pour the olive oil into the skillet. Place the skillet over medium heat and bring to a simmer. Cover tightly with foil or a lid, and transfer to the oven for 2 hours.

continued on page 46

the dough evenly to maintain a circle. Using a rolling pin, gently roll the dough out to a 12-inch circle.

Coat the bottom and sides of the skillet or baking dish using the 1 remaining tablespoon of olive oil.

Transfer the dough to the vessel, and allow the dough to fall to the bottom and cover the sides, stretching it a bit if necessary. Cut away any dough that falls over the rim of the vessel. Dust the dough with cornmeal, and cover with plastic wrap for 15 minutes.

Preheat the oven to 450°F. Remove the plastic wrap and transfer the dough-lined vessel to the oven and bake the crust alone for 10 minutes.

In a small mixing bowl, stir together tomatoes, olive oil, oregano, garlic powder, onion powder, and paprika.

Remove the crust from the oven. Lower the temperature to 375°F. Spread the mozzarella over the crust. Next, form a layer of the sausage, olives, and bell peppers. Then, pour the tomato purée mixture over all the fillings. Finally, evenly sprinkle the top with Parmesan cheese and transfer the vessel back to the oven. Bake for 30-35 minutes, or until the top is deep reddish gold and starting to crisp.

Remove the "pizza" from the oven and allow it to rest for 10 minutes before garnishing with basil and serving sloppy wedges of joy.

Mangled Pepperoni Pizza

USA

TOTAL TIME: 3 hours, or overnight plus 1 hour
CHARACTER: One Pot Meal, Main
VESSEL: 9 x 13 inch baking dish, or equivalent
SERVES: 6-8

> The one problem with pizza is that it's just too neat, too put together. No one and no food is that organized. Pizza should reflect life and embody a reality that we're all dealing with. Troubles at work? Bills to pay? Dog jumping on the guests? Glasses prescription getting worse? Hair thinning quickly? *My aching back!?* But, I digress. This is, finally, a (de)construction of pizza that will make you feel like your life is relatively tidy.
>
> —Greg

5 cups (about 1 lb) crusty bread, cubed
1 lb fresh mozzarella, diced
6 oz pepperoni, diced
4 Tbsp fresh basil, roughly chopped
5 eggs
2 cups half-and-half or milk
1 Tbsp dried oregano
3 Tbsp Parmesan cheese, grated or shredded, divided, plus extra for serving
1 tsp garlic powder
1 tsp salt
2 Tbsp extra-virgin olive oil, divided
1 cup tomato sauce, divided

Preheat the oven to 425°F. In a large mixing bowl, toss the bread cubes with mozzarella, pepperoni, and basil. In another mixing bowl, whisk together eggs, half-and-half or milk, oregano, 1 tablespoon of the Parmesan, garlic powder, and salt.

Coat the bottom and sides of a baking dish with 1 tablespoon of olive oil. Spread ½ cup of the tomato sauce in the bottom of the baking dish. Evenly pour the bread mixture into the baking dish and level out the top.

Slowly pour the egg mixture evenly over the bread mixture, being sure that some of the liquid reaches most, if not all, of the bread. Use the back of a wooden spoon, a clean hand, or spatula, to compress the whole mixture to ensure that the liquid is evenly distributed.

Spread the remaining ½ cup of the tomato sauce evenly across the top of the mixture. Sprinkle the top of the sauce with the remaining 2 tablespoons of Parmesan, and drizzle with the remaining 1 tablespoon of olive oil. Cover with plastic wrap and set aside for at least 2 hours (or in the refrigerator overnight).

Remove the plastic wrap and transfer the baking dish to the center rack of the oven. Bake for 40-45 minutes, or until the top begins to brown and get crusty.

Remove the casserole from the oven and allow it to cool for 10 minutes before slicing and serving. You may want to sprinkle some extra Parmesan over the finished product like any good pizza consumer.

Baked Green Bean Penne

USA

TOTAL TIME: 1 hour
CHARACTER: One Pot Meal
VESSEL: 9 x 13 inch baking dish, or equivalent
SERVES: 8-10

> When I was a kid, if it was a weekend, chances are we were at my Italian grandmother's house for Sunday gravy, lovingly loaded up with sweet fennel sausage and of course, meatballs. The table was adorned with incredible sides and a bevy of sensible accoutrement, bright, crisp green beans, ricotta for dolloping, and there was seemingly no end to extra gravy to take a plate over the top. Memories. Nearly all of them, here in one casserole.
>
> —Howie

4 qt water
1 lb penne pasta
2 Tbsp + 1 tsp salt, divided
12 oz fresh green beans, trimmed, cut into 1-inch segments
2 Tbsp extra-virgin olive oil, divided
½ lb bulk Italian sausage, or remove from casings
¼ lb ground beef
2 cloves garlic, minced
1 28-oz can pureed or crushed tomatoes
1 Tbsp dried oregano
½ tsp red pepper flakes (optional)
1 cup ricotta cheese
1 cup Parmesan cheese, shredded or grated
½ lb mozzarella, shredded
½ cup fresh basil leaves, roughly chopped

Preheat oven to 400°F.

In a large pot, bring water to a rolling boil over high heat. Add pasta and 2 tablespoons of salt. Cook for 7 minutes, stirring occasionally to ensure the pasta does not stick to the pot. Add green beans to the pot and continue to boil for 5 minutes. Drain the pasta and beans completely in a colander over the sink and set aside

Place a skillet over medium high heat. Add 1 tablespoon of olive oil. When oil begins to shimmer, add sausage and ground beef, breaking it up with a spatula into small bite-sized chunks. Sauté until the sausage browns, about 6–8 minutes.

Add garlic and cook until fragrant, about 30 seconds. Add the tomatoes, reduce the heat to medium-low, and simmer for 10 minutes, or until the sauce thickens.

continued on page 54

Empty the skillet contents into a large mixing bowl. Add the oregano, red pepper flakes (if using), ricotta, Parmesan, and remaining teaspoon of salt, and stir thoroughly. Add the drained pasta and beans to the bowl and fold in.

Coat the bottom and sides of a baking dish with the remaining 1 tablespoon of olive oil. Scrape the pasta mixture from the mixing bowl into the baking dish, and top with mozzarella. Transfer the into the oven and bake for 25–30 minutes, or until the cheese on top is golden brown. Allow the ziti to rest for 10 minutes before serving hot scoops topped with fresh basil.

Potato Crusted Spinach and Scallion Quiche

USA

TOTAL TIME: 1 hour, 20 minutes
CHARACTER: Main, Brunch
VESSEL: 8 x 8 inch baking dish, or equivalent
SERVES: 6-8

> This is a perfect dish to serve for your next brunch. Especially if your group of friends, like ours, means that you are trying to find something that's organic, gluten-free, vegetarian, Kosher, and Halal. Sorry vegans—I guess your invite got lost in the mail. I can't keep everyone happy.
>
> —Greg

- 2-3 (about 1½ lb) russet potatoes, peeled, shredded
- 3 Tbsp butter, divided
- 1½ tsp salt, divided
- 8 scallions, whites and greens separated, thinly sliced
- 1 clove garlic, minced
- 6 oz spinach, roughly chopped
- 3 cups milk
- ¼ tsp ground black pepper
- 6 eggs, beaten
- ¼ cup fresh basil, thinly sliced
- 2 cups sharp cheddar cheese
- 1 cup cherry tomatoes, halved

Preheat the oven to 425°F. Place potato shreds in a mixing bowl and cover with cold water.

Place 2 tablespoons of butter into a baking dish. Place dish in the oven for 3-5 minutes, or until the butter is melted and bubbling. Carefully remove the baking dish from the oven and swirl to ensure the butter coats the bottom.

Drain the potatoes well, squeezing handfuls in a sieve or towel to get the water out, and place them along the bottom of the baking dish. Using the back of a spoon or spatula, spread the potatoes evenly across the bottom, gently pressing to create a crust. Sprinkle with ½ teaspoon salt and place the dish back in the oven for 15 minutes, or until potatoes are browned. Remove the baking dish from the oven and lower the heat to 350°F.

continued on page 57

While the potatoes are browning, place a skillet over medium heat and add 1 tablespoon of butter. When the butter has melted and is starting to bubble, add the scallion whites and sauté for 1 minute. Add the garlic and continue to sauté for about 30 seconds, or until fragrant. Add the spinach, and continue to sauté until fully wilted, about 3-4 minutes.

Transfer the skillet contents to a large mixing bowl. Stir in the scallion greens, along with milk, the remaining 1 teaspoon of salt, and pepper. Whisk in eggs, then add basil and stir to combine.

Pour the egg and spinach mixture on top of the browned potato crust. Scatter cheese and tomatoes across the top. Place the casserole back in the oven, and bake for 45-50 minutes, or until quiche is fully set and the top begins to brown. Allow it to rest for 10 minutes, and either top with additional thinly sliced basil, or just dig in!

Shrimp Scampi Bulgur Bake

USA

TOTAL TIME: 45 minutes
CHARACTER: One Pot Meal, Main, Side
VESSEL: 8 x 8 inch baking dish, or equivalent
SERVES: 4-6

1 lb shrimp (30-40 ct), peeled, deveined
2 Tbsp extra-virgin olive oil, divided
1 Tbsp lemon juice
1 Tbsp lemon zest
1 clove garlic, minced
¼ cup dry white wine
1 tsp salt, divided
1 14½-oz can diced tomatoes
2 cups water
1 cup bulgur wheat (#2)
1 cup frozen corn kernels
½ cup parsley, divided

The title "Shrimp Scampi" always bothered me. "Scampi" is not shrimp, but rather another sea creature altogether! It's closer to a tiny lobster than it is to a shrimp. So, why the name? Shrimp, being much more available in the US than scampi, lead to shrimp being prepared as scampi would be in Italy! So "Shrimp in the style of Scampi" became "Shrimp Scampi." It also bothers me that it's always assumed to be served with pasta. Bulgur wheat is better for you and scrumptious. Class dismissed. And you're welcome.

—Howie

Preheat oven to 350°F. In a mixing bowl, combine shrimp, 1 tablespoon oil, lemon juice, zest, garlic, wine, and ½ teaspoon salt. Mix well, and set aside for 15 minutes.

Into the small pot, add the diced tomatoes, their juices, 2 cups water, and the remaining salt to a boil and reduce the heat to simmer. Cook for 15 minutes to make your tomato broth.

Coat the bottom and sides of a baking dish with remaining oil. Place an even layer of bulgur at the bottom of the baking dish, followed by a layer of corn kernels and ¼ cup parsley. Carefully pour the tomato broth over the corn, trying not to disturb the bulgur too much. Try for an even layer of tomatoes above the corn and parsley.

Place the shrimp in a single layer above the tomatoes. Drizzle the shrimp's marinade across the top of the casserole. Cover tightly with aluminum foil and transfer to the oven for 30-35 minutes, or until the shrimp has turned completely pink.

Remove the casserole from the oven, remove the foil, and sprinkle with the remaining parsley. Serve some shrimp with a scoop of tomato/corn/bulgur goodness.

Langoustine Mac and Cheese

USA

TOTAL TIME: 1 hour, 10 minutes
CHARACTER: One Pot Meal, Main, Side
VESSEL: 9 x 13 inch baking dish, or equivalent
SERVES: 6–8

Some years back, lobster macaroni and cheese was a huge fad, mostly at linen tablecloth, upscale restaurants. Then, when that faded, it became a huge fad at midscale, red-checkered tablecloth joints. Then, when that died down and food trucks started rolling out, it was a huge fad at *hugely faddish* mac and cheese trucks. Then, when that abated . . . we started to write this book. By the way, lobster is overrated. Frozen langoustine are cheaper, easier to deal with, and, in this kind of dish, better tasting.

—Howie

3 qt water
1 lb dry macaroni
3 Tbsp + 1 tsp salt, divided
2 eggs
1 cup heavy cream
1 cup milk
1 cup sour cream
1 tsp smoked paprika
½ tsp ground black pepper
½ tsp garlic powder
½ tsp onion powder
½ tsp chipotle powder (optional)
1 Tbsp dried oregano
4 cups (about 11 oz) sharp cheddar cheese, shredded, divided
½ lb langoustine tails, thawed if frozen
2 Tbsp extra-virgin olive oil, divided
⅓ cup bread crumbs

Preheat the oven to 375°F.

In a large pot, bring water to a rolling boil over high heat. Add pasta and 3 tablespoons salt. Cook for 10 minutes, stirring occasionally to ensure the pasta does not stick to the pot. Drain the pasta in a colander, and rinse with cold water to stop it from cooking further. Allow pasta to drain completely.

While the pasta is cooking, in a large mixing bowl, whisk together eggs, cream, milk, sour cream, the spices, and the remaining 1 teaspoon of salt. Add in the drained pasta, 3 cups of shredded cheese, langoustine tails, and mix thoroughly.

In a separate mixing bowl, stir together bread crumbs with the 1 tablespoon of olive oil and remaining cup of cheese.

Coat the bottom of a baking dish with 1 remaining tablespoon of olive oil. Pour the pasta mixture into the baking dish. Top the macaroni mixture with the bread crumb/cheese mixture.

Place the baking dish into the oven and bake for 40–45 minutes, or until the topping is golden and starting to brown. Remove the mac and cheese from the oven and allow it to cool for 10 minutes. Try to include some of the chewy top with each spooned serving.

Falafel Casserole

USA

TOTAL TIME: 1 hour, 45 minutes
CHARACTER: Main. Side
VESSEL: 9 x 13 inch baking dish, or equivalent
SERVES: 6-8

Many of my casserole ideas come from failed dinner parties. Have you ever tried to fry fresh falafel for 10 guests? Had your first batch fail utterly, requiring you to delay dinner for 20 minutes while you heat a new pot of oil? Wrapped your index finger in ice and gauze after placing it into said oil along with your second batch? You haven't? You are so smart! Given how smart you are, I'm sure you'll just make this lovely casserole, instead.

—Greg

CASSEROLE:

2 Tbsp extra-virgin olive oil, divided
3 15-oz cans of chickpeas, drained, rinsed, divided
3 shallots, minced (about 1 cup)
4 cloves garlic, minced
2 cups yogurt
¾ cup parsley, roughly chopped, divided
½ cup cilantro, roughly chopped
1 tsp lemon zest
1 tsp salt
1 tsp ground cumin
½ tsp ground coriander
½ tsp dried red chile flakes (optional)
1 cup plain bread crumbs
¼ cup Parmesan cheese

TAHINI SAUCE:

½ cup tahini
Juice of 1 lemon
½ cup water
½ tsp salt

Preheat the oven to 375°F. Prepare a baking dish by coating the bottom and sides with 1 tablespoon of olive oil.

In a large mixing bowl, add half of the chickpeas and crush them into a rough paste using a potato masher or a large fork. Then, add the remaining whole chickpeas, shallots, garlic, yogurt, ½ cup of parsley, cilantro, lemon zest, salt, cumin, coriander, and, if you are using them, the chile flakes. Stir to combine well. In a smaller mixing bowl, combine the bread crumbs and Parmesan cheese.

Layer the chickpea mixture across the casserole dish. Sprinkle the bread crumb mixture, covering the entire casserole. Drizzle with the remaining 1 tablespoon of extra-virgin olive oil. Transfer the baking dish to the oven and bake for 40-45 minutes, or until the top is golden.

While the casserole is baking, combine the tahini, lemon juice, water, and salt in a large bowl. Whisk until completely smooth.

Remove the casserole from the oven, garnish with the remaining ¼ cup of parsley, and serve hot or warm, with the tahini sauce. Goes great with a lemon-dressed salad!

Buffalo Chicken Casserole

USA

TOTAL TIME: 1 hour
CHARACTER: Main
VESSEL: 9 x 13 inch baking dish, or equivalent
SERVES: 6–8

Just after college, Howie and I went on a road trip that brought us through Buffalo. I remember the brick buildings, so different from what I'd see in California. I remember Niagara Falls and the "Maid of the Mist." What I don't remember are any Buffalo wings. I mean, I'm sure that they were around, but we just didn't think to eat any. I have such regrets!

—Greg

¼ cup vegetable oil, divided
½ cup Buffalo-style hot sauce
2 tsp onion powder
1 tsp garlic powder
1 Tbsp mild chile powder or paprika
1 tsp ground black pepper
½ tsp salt
2-3 (about 1½ lb) russet potatoes, cut into ½ inch slices
2 Tbsp butter
1 medium onion, diced
1 green bell pepper, diced
2 stalks celery, diced
2 lb chicken breasts, boneless, skinless, diced
3 cups sharp cheddar cheese, shredded
Blue cheese or ranch salad dressing, for serving

Preheat the oven to 450°F.

In a mixing bowl, prepare a sauce by combining 3 tablespoons of oil, hot sauce, onion powder, garlic powder, chile powder, black pepper, and salt. Stir until well combined.

In a separate mixing bowl, combine potato slices with a third of the prepared sauce. Toss to coat. Coat a baking dish with 1 tablespoon of vegetable oil. Place the dressed potatoes along the bottom of the pan, covering as much of the pan as possible but keeping it to one layer. It is okay to overlap slices. Transfer the baking dish to the oven and roast for 30 minutes, or until the bottom of the potatoes have browned.

continued on page 66

While the potatoes are roasting, place a skillet over medium-high heat. Add butter. Once the butter is melted, add onion, bell pepper, celery, and sauté until the onion begins to brown, about 8-10 minutes. Add chicken and sauté until just browned, about another 3-4 minutes. Finally, add the remaining sauce and cook for another minute. Turn off the heat and set aside.

When the potatoes are roasted, remove the pan from the oven and lower the temperature to 350°F.

On top of the potatoes, layer half of the skillet mixture, then cover with ½ of the cheese. Repeat the layering with the remainder of the chicken and the last of the cheese. Return to the oven and bake for 15 minutes, or until the cheese is melted and beginning to brown. You may want to finish under the broiler for extra browning.

Serve by drizzling with blue cheese or ranch dressing. Feel free to class it up by garnishing with a stalk or two of raw celery.

Chicken Umami Cobbler

USA

TOTAL TIME: 1 hour, 30 minutes
CHARACTER: One Pot Meal, Main
VESSEL: 9 x 13 inch baking dish, or equivalent
SERVES: 6–8

Where were you when you first heard about *umami*? This page? Umami is considered to be the *fifth* taste or savory (for lack of a better term) after sour, sweet, salty, and bitter. There are a number of ingredients that have a native earthy, umami quality. Here, we turn a humble chicken cobbler up a few notches with mushrooms, tomato paste, soy sauce, and aged cheddar cheese. It's hard to know which is more fun. Tasting umami. Or saying it. Try saying it out loud and not smiling. No, really. I'm waiting . . .

—Howie

FILLING:

3 Tbsp extra-virgin olive oil, divided
1 large onion, diced
1 large carrot, diced
2 stalks celery, thinly sliced
2 tsp salt, divided
1 tsp black pepper
10 oz fresh cremini, shiitake, or other mushrooms, minced
2 Tbsp tomato paste
½ cup all-purpose flour
2 Tbsp soy sauce
2 cups chicken stock or broth
1 cup frozen peas
1 Tbsp dried oregano
¼ cup parsley, chopped
¼ cup heavy cream
1½ lb chicken breast filets, boneless, skinless
2 tsp smoked paprika

BISCUIT TOPPING:

2½ cups flour
½ tsp baking soda
1 Tbsp baking powder
½ tsp salt
1 tsp sugar
1 cup aged cheddar cheese, shredded
⅓ cup Greek-style yogurt
1 cup milk
⅓ cup + 2 Tbsp extra virgin olive oil, divided

continued on page 69

Preheat the oven to 400°F.

Place a skillet over medium-low heat and add 2 tablespoons of olive oil. When the oil begins to shimmer, add onion, celery, carrot, 1 teaspoon of salt, black pepper, and sauté until the onion begins to caramelize, about 12-15 minutes. Add mushrooms and tomato paste, and continue to sauté for an additional 10 minutes, or until the mushrooms have begun to brown.

Add in flour and stir until you can no longer see white, then sauté for 2 additional minutes. Add soy sauce, stock, peas, oregano, parsley, and bring to a boil. Lower the heat to a simmer and stir in the cream. Allow the filling to simmer for 25-30 minutes, while you prepare the chicken.

Place the chicken on a sheet pan and coat with paprika, remaining 1 teaspoon of salt, and remaining 1 tablespoon of olive oil. Transfer the sheet pan to the oven and roast for 20 minutes. Remove the chicken from the oven and shred with a knife or in a stand mixer with the paddle attachment.

Add the shredded chicken to the skillet and stir it into the filling. Carefully transfer the filling to a baking dish and allow the filling to cool while you make the biscuit topping.

In a large mixing bowl, whisk together flour, baking soda, baking powder, salt, and sugar. Mix in the cheese, and be sure there are no cheese clumps. In a separate mixing bowl, whisk together yogurt, milk, and ⅓ cup of olive oil. Pour the wet ingredients into the dry and mix well with clean hands until dough forms.

Dust the counter or a board with flour, and transfer your dough from the bowl. Dust the top of the dough with more flour and begin to flatten and mold together with a floured hand and/or a rolling pin. Work the dough until it is ¾ of an inch thick. Cut out dough rounds with a 3-inch biscuit cutter or the top of a 3-inch wide glass, and place the dough rounds on top of the filling in the baking dish. Drizzle the remaining 2 tablespoons of olive oil over the biscuit dough.

Transfer the baking dish to the oven and bake until biscuits are starting to brown, about 20-25 minutes. Remove the cobbler from the oven and scoop servings that include a biscuit and a healthy dose of filling.

Tomato Cobbler

USA

TOTAL TIME: 1 hour, 5 minutes
CHARACTER: One Pot Meal, Main, Side
VESSEL: 8 x 8 inch baking dish, 4 2-cup ramekins, or equivalent
SERVES: 4-6

Cherry tomatoes are cute, punchy, juicy, sweet, and awesome, but they often get relegated to the staidest part of the meal . . . the salad! Eeek! What a waste! This dish celebrates the little ruby beauties and pairs them with a genius foil of a cheesy biscuit topping. Enjoy the non-saladiness of it!

—Greg

FILLING:

2 Tbsp flour
3 Tbsp extra-virgin olive oil
2 lb grape or cherry tomatoes, halved
2 scallions, thinly sliced
1 large red bell pepper, roasted, peeled, diced
1 tsp salt
½ tsp sugar
½ tsp ground black pepper
1 tsp garlic powder
2 tsp dried oregano

BISCUIT TOPPING:

2½ cups flour
½ tsp baking soda
1 Tbsp baking powder
½ tsp salt
1 tsp sugar
1 cup Parmesan cheese, grated or shredded
⅓ cup Greek yogurt
1 cup milk
⅓ cup + 2 Tbsp extra-virgin olive oil, divided

Preheat the oven to 350°F.

To make the filling, in a large mixing bowl, whisk flour and olive oil together. Then, add the remaining filling ingredients to the bowl and mix well. Transfer the tomato mixture to a baking dish or distribute into ramekins.

continued on page 72

To make the topping, in a large mixing bowl, whisk together the flour, baking soda, baking powder, salt, and sugar. Mix in the cheese, making sure there are no cheese clumps. In a separate mixing bowl, whisk together the yogurt, milk, and ⅓ cup of olive oil. Pour the wet ingredients into the dry and mix well with clean hands until dough forms.

Dust the counter or a board with flour, and transfer your dough from the bowl. Dust the top of the dough with more flour and begin to flatten and mold together with a floured hand and/or a rolling pin. Work the dough until it is ¾ of an inch thick. Cut 3-inch dough squares and place on top of the filling in the baking dish or one per ramekin. Drizzle the remaining 2 tablespoons of olive oil over the biscuit dough.

Transfer the baking vessel/s to the oven and bake until biscuits are starting to brown, about 35-40 minutes. Remove the cobbler from the oven and allow it to cool for 15 minutes. If using a baking dish, scoop servings and include a biscuit. If using ramekins, serve to individuals or couples.

Cornbread and Biscuit "Stuffing"

USA

TOTAL TIME: Overnight, plus 2 hours, 40 minutes
CHARACTER: Side
VESSEL: 9 x 13 inch baking dish, or equivalent
SERVES: 8-10

> Some call me overindulgent. I like a veggie burger *with* a hamburger on the same bun. I'll add hot fudge, caramel, *and* butterscotch onto a sundae. I love a good deep fried mac and cheese. Chicken and waffles with maple syrup *and* hot sauce? Sign me up! But the best example of this rather attractive part of my character is in my affinity for a terrific *overdoing-it* Southern "stuffing." Why use cornbread alone when you can kick it up a tier with buttery buttermilk biscuits? Please join me on the overindulgence train, would you?
>
> —Howie

2 lb prepared cornbread, from page 37
4 3-inch buttermilk biscuits, Biscuit Topping from page 10
2 Tbsp butter
10 oz cremini, white button, or shiitake mushrooms, stemmed and thinly sliced
2 Tbsp extra-virgin olive oil, divided
3 stalks celery, diced
1 large green bell pepper, diced
2 tsp salt, divided
1 tsp ground black pepper
1 tsp onion powder
1 tsp garlic powder
2 tsp dried or fresh thyme leaves
5 scallions, thinly sliced
¼ cup parsley, roughly chopped
1 large egg
4 cups vegetable or mushroom broth, cooled
½ cup milk

To make the biscuits from the Biscuits and Red Gravy Casserole recipe from page 10: Bake the dough squares on a greased sheet pan in a 400°F oven for 20-25 minutes or until golden.

To make the cornbread from the Cajun Okra and Tomato Bake recipe on page 37: Bake the batter in a cast iron skillet or baking dish in a 400°F oven for 35-40 minutes or until golden. Leave the cornbread and biscuits on the counter, uncovered, overnight to dry out.

continued on page 75

Preheat the oven to 375°F. Place a skillet over medium heat. Add butter. When the butter has melted, add the mushrooms and sauté until they give off their water and start to brown, about 10 minutes. Transfer the mushrooms to a large mixing bowl. To the skillet, add 1 tablespoon of olive oil, celery, bell pepper, 1 teaspoon of salt, pepper, onion powder, garlic powder, and thyme. Sauté until the celery is almost translucent, about 6–8 minutes. Transfer the skillet contents to the mixing bowl with the mushrooms.

To this mixing bowl, mix in the scallions and parsley, then roughly crumble the cornbread and biscuits on top. In a separate bowl, whisk together the egg, broth, milk, and remaining 1 teaspoon of salt. Pour the broth mixture into the bread mixture. Stir to combine until the liquid is fully absorbed.

Coat the bottom and sides of a baking dish with the remaining 1 tablespoon of olive oil. Pour the contents of the mixing bowl into a baking dish, gently pressing to ensure everything fits in one solid layer.

Cover with plastic wrap and allow the baking dish to sit on the counter for an hour, undisturbed.

Place the baking dish onto the center rack of the oven and bake for 50–60 minutes, or until the top is golden and crusty. Remove the "stuffing" from the oven and allow it to rest for 5-10 minutes before serving. This "stuffing" also goes great with a vegetable or meat gravy.

Scalloped Potatoes and Sweet Potatoes

USA

TOTAL TIME: 1 hour, 35 minutes
CHARACTER: Side
VESSEL: 9 x 13 inch baking dish, or equivalent
SERVES: 6-8

Scalloped potatoes have always been a household pleasure. But, when I was growing up, we could only afford white potatoes. No, hold on. When I was growing up, sweet potatoes hadn't been cultivated yet. Wait, that can't be right. When I was growing up, we loved eating monotone foods. None of this sounds correct. Maybe we were waiting for high definition TV? This is a gorgeous dish.

—Howie

3 Tbsp extra-virgin olive oil, divided
2-3 (about 1½ lb) russet potatoes, peeled, sliced ⅛-inch thick (a mandoline helps)
1½ lb purple or orange sweet potatoes, peeled, sliced ⅛-inch thick
1½ cups Monterey Jack cheese, shredded
1½ cups Parmesan cheese, grated or shredded
3 tsp dried oregano, divided
3 cups half-and-half or cream
3 large eggs
2 tsp salt
1 tsp ground black pepper
1 tsp garlic powder
1 tsp ancho or other chile powder

Preheat the oven to 375°F. Using a pastry brush or paper towel, coat the bottom and sides of a baking dish with 1 tablespoon of olive oil.

Form a layer using a third of the potato and sweet potato slices along the bottom of the baking dish, overlapping them like shingles. Sprinkle ½ cup of each cheese and 1 teaspoon of oregano over the potatoes. Repeat with another layer of a third of the potato and sweet potato slices, ½ cup of both cheeses, and 1 teaspoon of oregano. Place one last layer of the remaining potato and sweet potato.

In a large mixing bowl, whisk together half-and-half or cream, eggs, salt, pepper, garlic powder, and chile powder. Slowly pour the cream mixture over the potatoes, giving it some time to fall to the bottom of the baking dish and surround its contents. Sprinkle the remaining 1 teaspoon of oregano across the top.

Cover the baking dish tightly with aluminum foil and transfer to the oven and bake for 40 minutes. Remove the baking dish from the oven and discard the foil. Sprinkle the top of the casserole with the remaining ½ cup of both cheeses, drizzle with the remaining 2 tablespoons of olive oil, and return to the oven, uncovered, for an additional 20-25 minutes or until the cheese melts and the top begins to brown.

Remove the casserole from the oven and allow it to cool for 10-15 minutes before slicing and serving warm.

Creamed Sweet Onions

USA

TOTAL TIME: 1 hour, 25 minutes
CHARACTER: Side
VESSEL: 9 x 13 inch baking dish, or equivalent
SERVES: 6-8

> The humble onion. It's in nearly everything we eat. But, it seldom takes center stage. Like that one character actor who you just can't place, but always plays an intimidating yet witty hit man in mob movies. If he were, even once, given the spotlight, I'm sure he'd be amazing! Just like this dish where the onion takes its well-deserved lead role.
>
> —Greg

2 Tbsp extra-virgin olive oil, divided
4 large Vidalia or other sweet onions, cut into ½-inch thick cross-section slices (visible concentric rings)
1½ tsp salt, divided
1 cup heavy cream
¼ cup sour cream
1 tsp garlic powder
1 tsp smoked paprika
1 tsp ground black pepper
2 tsp dried oregano
1 cup Parmesan cheese, grated

Preheat the oven to 400°F.

Using 1 tablespoon of olive oil, coat the bottom and sides of a baking dish. Lay onion slices flat along the bottom. Drizzle with the remaining 1 tablespoon of olive oil, and sprinkle with 1 teaspoon of salt. Cover the baking dish tightly with aluminum foil, transfer to the oven, and roast for 45-50 minutes, or until the onions are very soft. Remove the baking dish from the oven and discard the foil.

In a mixing bowl, whisk together heavy cream, sour cream, garlic powder, paprika, pepper, oregano, and the remaining ½ teaspoon of salt. Pour the cream mixture over the onions and sprinkle Parmesan across the top. Return the baking dish to the oven and continue to roast for an additional 20-25 minutes or until the onions and cheese have begun to brown.

Remove the creamed onions from the oven and serve hot. Be sure to include a bit of the sauce with every serving.

Chesapeake Crabby "Stuffing"

USA

TOTAL TIME: 2 hours, 30 minutes
CHARACTER: Side
VESSEL: 11 x 15 baking dish, or equivalent
SERVES: 10-12

> I'm the guy who eats with his hands *only* if the food is shielded by a dry starch. Can I get an amen? Burritos and tacos, check. BLT, check. Chinese steamed buns, check. Whenever I've been faced with the prospect of sitting at a picnic table, overlooking the bay, and handed a tray of steaming hot ruby-red crabs, a tiny hammer and a bib . . . Well, I'll let you imagine my reaction. This "stuffing" is great, but please, for the sake of civilization, serve it with a fork.
>
> —Howie

1 Tbsp butter
3 Tbsp extra-virgin olive oil, divided
1 large onion, diced
3 stalks celery, diced
2 tsp salt, divided
1 tsp ground black pepper
1 tsp garlic powder
1 tsp chile powder
1 Tbsp dried oregano
1 4-oz can roasted green chiles, diced
¼ cup parsley, roughly chopped
8 oz ham, diced
1½-lb loaf crusty bread, cut into 1-inch cubes
8 oz crab meat, backfin or lump
1 large egg
3 cups chicken or seafood broth, cooled
½ cup milk

Place a skillet over medium heat. Add butter and 2 tablespoons of olive oil. When the butter has melted, add the onion, celery, 1 teaspoon of salt, and the remaining seasonings, and sauté until the onion is translucent, about 6-8 minutes. Transfer the contents to a large mixing bowl.

To this mixing bowl, stir in the chiles, parsley, ham, and bread cubes. Then, gently fold in crab.

Coat the bottom and sides of a baking dish with the remaining 1 tablespoon of olive oil. Scrape the bread mixture into the baking dish, making sure to evenly distribute it across the dish.

In a mixing bowl, whisk the egg, broth, milk, and the remaining 1 teaspoon of salt. Slowly pour the liquid over the mixture in the baking dish, being sure that some of the liquid reaches most, if not all, of the bread. Use a clean hand, the back of a wooden spoon, or spatula, to compress the whole mixture to ensure that the liquid is evenly distributed.

Cover with plastic wrap and transfer the baking dish to the refrigerator for one hour.

Preheat the oven to 375°F. Remove the baking dish from the refrigerator, uncover, and transfer to the center rack of the oven. Bake for 45-55 minutes, or until the top is begins to brown and get crusty. Remove the "stuffing" from the oven and allow it to rest for 5-10 minutes before serving. Smothering a healthy scoop of this with gravy is a special treat!

Healthier Than It Tastes "Stuffing"

USA

TOTAL TIME: 1 hour
CHARACTER: Side
VESSEL: 9 x 13 inch baking dish, or equivalent
SERVES: 8-10

I remember coming home from sleepaway camp one summer, to find that the chocolate chip cookies were now whole grain carob bars, and the cola was now seltzer. This was not a huge surprise, as Mom was always trying to figure out ways to have us eat healthier. Mostly, this sucked—I mean have you ever eaten a carob bar? But, one Thanksgiving she decided to supplement a small package of stuffing mix with a metric ton of veggies. Surprisingly, it was much, much better than ordinary stuffing. I invite you to give it a try yourself!

—Greg

1 lb crusty bread, diced
3 Tbsp vegetable oil, divided
1 large onion, diced
1 tsp salt
1 tsp ground black pepper
1 tsp paprika
3 garlic cloves, minced
2 stalks celery, thinly sliced
1 head cauliflower, grated
1 medium carrot, grated
3 medium zucchini, grated
1 tsp dried thyme
1 tsp dried oregano
1 tsp dried sage
2 cups chicken broth

Preheat the oven to 350°F.

Place the bread cubes on a sheet pan and toast them in the oven for 10-12 minutes. You know what toast looks like.

While the bread is toasting, place a skillet over medium-high heat. Add 1 tablespoon of oil. When the oil begins to shimmer, add the onion, salt, pepper, and paprika. Sauté until the onions begin to turn translucent, about 6–8 minutes. Turn the heat up to high, and add the garlic, celery, cauliflower, carrot, zucchini, thyme, oregano, and sage. Sauté for another 5-7 minutes, until the vegetables soften and start to brown.

Transfer the skillet contents to a large mixing bowl. Add toast cubes and broth to the vegetable mixture, and fold to combine.

continued on page 84

Add the remaining 2 tablespoons of oil to the bottom of a baking dish. Place the empty oiled dish into the oven for 5 minutes. When the oil is very hot, remove the dish from the oven and spoon the stuffing mixture from the mixing bowl into the baking dish. It should sizzle as it hits the oil. Using a spatula, even out the top of the stuffing.

Place the baking dish back in the oven for 30 minutes, or until the top is crisp and lightly brown. Allow the stuffing to cool for 10 minutes before digging in!

Tortilla Chicken Stack
(Tlayuda)
MEXICO

TOTAL TIME: 1 hour
CHARACTER: One Pot Meal, Main, Side
VESSEL: 12 inch cast iron skillet, or other oven-safe skillet
SERVES: 6-8

1 lb chicken breast halves, boneless, skinless
3 Tbsp extra-virgin olive oil, divided
2 tsp salt, divided
1 white onion, diced
1 tsp garlic powder
2 tsp ancho or other chile powder
2 tsp cumin
1 tsp ground black pepper
2 15-oz cans black beans, rinsed, drained
¼ cup vegetable or chicken broth
½ cup sour cream
2 Tbsp milk
3 large flour tortillas
1½ cups mozzarella or Monterey Jack cheese
1 cup lettuce, shredded
1 cup cherry tomatoes, halved

Continuing along the theme of *Howie didn't know Mexican food for half of his life*, I used to "run for the border," and go to this fast food taco place to get their "Mexican pizza." What can I say? I was a sad, confused man of 20 years. As it turns out, there is indeed a "Mexican pizza," if you will, from Oaxaca called *tlayuda*—a griddled crispy tortilla topped with all the good stuff, served in wedges or rolled up like a burrito. Here, we adapt it and stack it like a lasagna because it serves a crowd, it adds a variety of textures, and it's delicious.

—Howie

Preheat the oven to 400°F. Arrange a rack on the lower third of the oven.

Coat the chicken with 1 tablespoon of olive oil, and 1 teaspoon of salt. Massage the chicken to spread both evenly. Transfer the chicken to a roasting pan and into the oven for 25 minutes.

While the chicken cooks, place a skillet over medium-high heat. Add 1 tablespoon of olive oil. When the oil begins to shimmer, add the onion and sauté for 6-8 minutes, or until the edges begin to brown. Add the garlic powder, chile powder, cumin, remaining salt, and pepper, and continue to sauté for 2 minutes. Transfer the onion mixture and the drained beans to a blender or food

continued on page 87

processor and wipe out the skillet. Add broth to the blender or food processor and purée. Set the bean purée aside.

In a mixing bowl combine the sour cream and milk; set aside. Remove the chicken from the oven, and either dice with a knife, or shred with two forks or in a stand mixer with the paddle attachment.

Using a pastry brush or paper towel, coat the bottom and sides of the skillet with the remaining 1 tablespoon of olive oil. Place 1 tortilla at the bottom of the skillet. Spread half of the bean purée across the top of the tortilla. Scatter half of the chicken atop the bean purée, followed by ½ cup of your cheese.

Place another tortilla atop the cheese. Repeat the layers above, remaining half of the purée, remaining half of the chicken, and ½ cup of the mozzarella. Place the last tortilla on top, then the final ½ cup of the mozzarella. Transfer the skillet to the lower third of the oven and roast for 15–20 minutes, until the cheese is melted, the top is golden brown, and the top edges are slightly crispy.

Remove the skillet from the oven. Allow the tlayuda to rest for 5 minutes. Top with lettuce, tomato, and drizzle the sour cream mixture to finish it off. Serve wedges directly from the skillet.

Ahi Tuna Tower

USA

TOTAL TIME: 1 hour, 10 minutes
CHARACTER: One Pot Meal
VESSEL: 8 x 8 inch baking dish, or equivalent
SERVES: 6-8

Hold on a minute. Do you mean to tell me that a casserole doesn't have to be cooked at all? Yes, that is what I'm saying. *But you told us in your opening manifesto of this beautiful book that a casserole by definition had to spend at least some time in the oven.* You should know better than to listen to me. *Do you often talk to yourself?* Yes. It helps. This beauty of a *casserole* is the result of years of diligent and delicious study. Investigations into perfect combinations of flavors, textures, and emotions have led me to the ideal Japan-inspired composition. Where it does not spend time in the oven, it is baked in love. Whammo!

—Howie

CASSEROLE:

- 1 cup Japanese or other short grain rice, uncooked
- 2 lb sushi-grade Ahi tuna, diced
- 3 Tbsp soy sauce
- 1 Tbsp sugar
- 3 Tbsp rice vinegar
- 1 tsp vegetable, canola, or other neutral-flavored oil
- 1 lb jumbo lump crab meat
- 2 avocados, peeled, pitted, diced

SAUCE:

- 1 cup mayonnaise
- ¾ cup sriracha-style hot sauce
- 2 Tbsp black sesame seeds

Cook the rice according to package directions, approximately 30 minutes. Meanwhile, in a mixing bowl, combine the tuna and soy sauce. Allow the mixture to marinate while you await the rice.

Once the rice is cooked, transfer it to a cool, flat surface with a rim, such as a clean baking dish. While the rice is hot, sprinkle it with sugar and then the rice vinegar and stir to combine. Stir occasionally for the next 30 minutes to help it cool and so the rice doesn't clump up.

To make the sauce, combine the mayonnaise with the hot sauce in a small mixing bowl. Stir to blend completely. Set aside.

Using a paper towel, coat the bottom and sides of a baking dish with oil. In the bottom of the baking dish, spread an even layer using all the tuna. Use the back of a spoon or a clean hand to press the layer flat. Then create a similar layer using all the crab, followed by a layer of the avocadoes. Lastly, cover the top with an even layer of the seasoned rice. The contents should be flush with the top of the baking dish, if not very close.

Find a (liftable) cutting board or flat platter larger than the baking dish. Place the board or platter upside down on top of the baking dish and carefully flip, so the baking dish ends up on top. Slowly unmold the Tuna Tower. It should separate from the baking dish smoothly.

Pour the spicy mayonnaise sauce across the top of the Tower, sprinkle with sesame seeds, and serve in heaps. Try to include all layers!

Garden Lasagna

USA

TOTAL TIME: 1 hour, 15 minutes
CHARACTER: Main, Side
VESSEL: 9 x 13 inch baking dish, or equivalent
SERVES: 4–6

2 Tbsp extra-virgin olive oil, divided
1 large onion, diced
2 stalks celery, sliced thinly
2 carrots, grated
2 cloves garlic, minced
2 tsp salt, divided
12 oz baby spinach
¾ cup parsley, chopped
1 red bell pepper, roasted, peeled, diced
1 28-oz can pureed tomatoes
1 Tbsp dried oregano
9 oz no-boil (oven-ready) lasagna noodles
1 lb mozzarella cheese, shredded
½ cup bread crumbs
½ cup Parmesan cheese, grated

When Greg and I were writing our previous cookbook, *One Pan to Rule Them All*, he developed a recipe for a cheeseless lasagna and I was skeptical that he could pull it off. *What's a lasagna without cheese?*, I openly mocked. Actually, it was with immense pleasure that I was swayed in his seemingly blasphemous direction. It was delectable and deceptively delicious. I enjoyed it so much that I wondered what would happen if I used the same combination of magic and put the gosh darn cheese back in. Here it is. *Take that, Matza!*

—Howie

Preheat the oven to 350°F.

Place a skillet over medium heat. Add 1 tablespoon of the olive oil. When the oil begins to shimmer, add the onion and sauté 6–8 minutes, until translucent. Add the celery, carrots, garlic, and 1 teaspoon of salt, and sauté another 2 minutes. Add spinach, stirring occasionally, until the spinach is completely wilted, about 4 minutes. Remove the mixture to a mixing bowl. Add the parsley, red pepper, and stir to distribute them evenly.

In a separate mixing bowl, combine the pureed tomatoes, oregano, and the remaining 1 teaspoon of salt.

In a baking dish, spread 1 cup of the tomato mixture over the bottom. Over that, add a layer of the noodles. Then layer one-quarter of the vegetable mixture, then one-quarter of the mozzarella. Repeat three more times (tomato, noodles, vegetables, mozzarella). Cover tightly with aluminum foil. Bake for 30 minutes.

While the lasagna is baking, in a mixing bowl, combine bread crumbs, Parmesan cheese, and the remaining 1 tablespoon of olive oil.

Remove the lasagna from the oven, uncover, sprinkle bread crumb cheese mixture across the top. Return the uncovered baking dish to oven for 12–15 minutes, or until the top is lightly browned. Allow the lasagna to rest for 5 minutes before slicing and serving.

No-Noodle Zucchini Lasagna

USA

TOTAL TIME: 2 hours, 30 minutes
CHARACTER: One Pot Meal, Main
VESSEL: 9 x 13 inch baking dish, or equivalent
SERVES: 4-6

2 Tbsp extra-virgin olive oil, divided
1 large onion, diced
1½ tsp salt, divided
2 cloves garlic, minced
1 lb ground beef
1 cup mushrooms, thinly sliced
¾ cup red wine
1 15-oz can pureed tomatoes
½ cup water
1 6-oz can tomato paste
1½ tsp dried basil
½ tsp dried thyme
½ tsp dried oregano
½ tsp ground black pepper
1 bay leaf
5 medium zucchini (about 2 lb), cut into ⅛ inch-thick strips
12 oz ricotta cheese
12 oz mozzarella cheese, shredded
1 cup Parmesan cheese, shredded or grated

Have you ever grown a zucchini plant? One year, my genius father decided it would be great to put three of them in the backyard. We had zucchini coming out of our ears all summer. We roasted it with tomatoes. We baked it in bread. We gave it to neighbors. We whittled it into art projects. And still, it kept coming. This casserole was one of the innovations of that summer. Unlike my art projects, it was good enough that we kept it around, even in subsequent summers when we were smart enough to leave the squash growing to the professionals.

—Greg

To make the sauce, place a skillet over medium heat. Add 1 tablespoon of the olive oil. When the oil begins to shimmer, add the onion and 1 teaspoon salt and sauté 6–8 minutes, or until translucent. Add the garlic and cook until fragrant, about 30 seconds. Add the beef and mushrooms and sauté until the meat is browned, about 6-8 minutes. Add the wine and scrape the bottom of the pan to free the browned bits.

Once the wine has bubbled for a minute, add the tomatoes, water, tomato paste, basil, thyme, oregano, pepper, and bay leaf. Reduce the heat to low and simmer, uncovered, for 30-45minutes—the longer it cooks, the better it will taste.

While the sauce cooks, preheat the oven to 375°F. When the sauce is done, remove the bay leaf.

Prepare a baking dish by coating it with the remaining 1 tablespoon of olive oil. Using a third of the zucchini, create a layer of overlapping slices to cover the bottom of the baking dish. Use a third of the ricotta to spread dollops across the layer of zucchini. Use a third of the mozzarella to sprinkle a layer across the ricotta. Top the cheese with a third of the meat sauce. Repeat this twice more: zucchini, ricotta, mozzarella, meat sauce. Top with Parmesan cheese.

Transfer the baking dish to the oven and bake for 45-50 minutes, or until top is beginning to brown. Remove the lasagna from the oven and allow it to rest for 15 minutes before serving up heaping blocks of cheesy goodness.

Santa Fe Corn Casserole

USA

TOTAL TIME: 1 hour, 10 minutes
CHARACTER: Side
VESSEL: 9 x 13 inch baking dish, or equivalent
SERVES: 6–8

> I love the Chinese culinary mindscape. One of the most entertaining dishes is called "tiger skin peppers." The chef fries two types of peppers that look identical! One is sweet and the other is very (very) spicy. From one bite to the next, you are biting into a mystery. A mystery with potentially dire consequences! With this dish, you can wow your guests in a similar, albeit more gentle way, by strategically grouping the mild and hot green chiles across the casserole. Don't be boring.
>
> —Greg

1 cup yellow cornmeal
⅓ cup all-purpose flour
¼ cup sugar
¼ tsp baking soda
½ tsp baking powder
1 cup buttermilk
½ tsp salt
1 clove garlic, minced
1 16-oz can creamed corn
2 large eggs, beaten
¼ cup + 1 Tbsp extra-virgin olive oil
1 4-oz can diced green chilies, mild
1 4-oz can diced green chilies, hot
8 oz Monterey Jack cheese, shredded
Sour cream and/or hot sauce for garnish

Preheat the oven to 375°F. In a large mixing bowl, stir together cornmeal, flour, sugar, baking soda, baking powder, buttermilk, salt, garlic, corn, eggs, and ¼ cup of olive oil. Only stir until everything is barely but evenly combined (no flour streaks). Some lumps are okay.

Coat the bottom and sides of a baking dish with the remaining 1 tablespoon of olive oil. Pour the batter into the baking dish. On top of the batter, place a layer of hot and mild peppers, placed so one bite will be hot and the other sweet. Top the peppers with shredded cheese.

Bake in the oven for 45–50 minutes or until the cheese on top is crisp and browned. Remove from oven and allow to cool for 10 minutes.

Serve warm scoops directly from the baking dish. Top with sour cream or hot sauce.

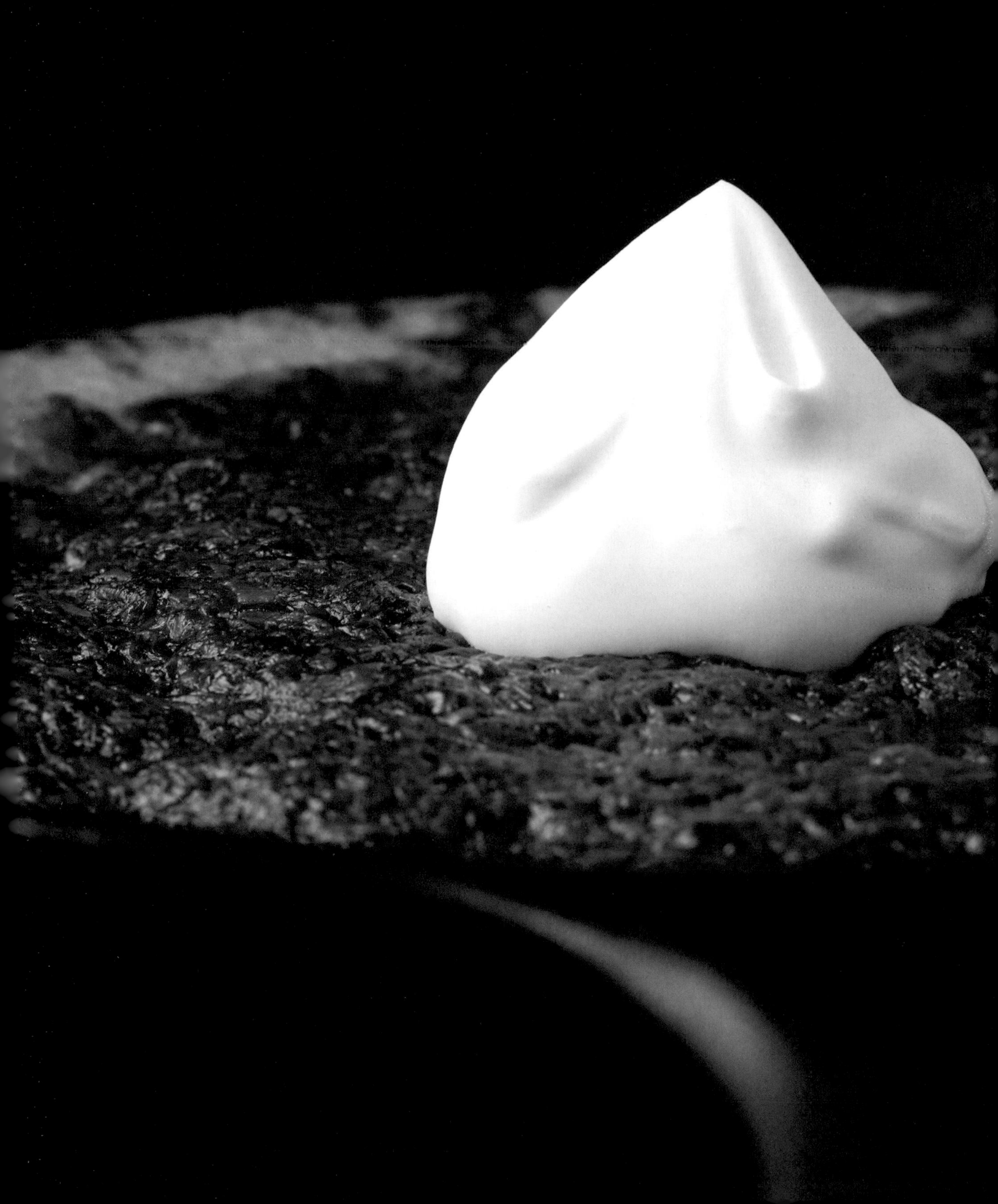

Southwestern Rice and Beans Casserole

USA

TOTAL TIME: 1 hour
CHARACTER: One Pot Meal
VESSEL: 10 inch cast iron skillet with a lid, or other oven-safe skillet with a lid
SERVES: 4–6

> For when Taco Tuesday just seems like too much work.
>
> —Greg

2 cups vegetable broth or water
2 Tbsp soy sauce
1 cup canned diced tomatoes, with juices
2 15-oz cans black beans, rinsed, drained
1 cup frozen corn kernels
1 tsp salt
½ tsp paprika
½ tsp garlic powder
½ tsp onion powder
½ tsp ancho or other chile powder
1 cup jasmine or other long grain rice, uncooked
6 oz cheddar cheese, shredded
Guacamole and sour cream for serving

Preheat the oven to 375°F. Place a skillet over medium heat. Add the broth or water, soy sauce, tomatoes, black beans, corn, salt, paprika, garlic powder, onion powder, and chile powder. Bring to a boil, then lower the heat to a simmer. Add the rice and stir to distribute evenly. Cover and transfer the skillet to the oven for 30 minutes.

Remove the skillet from the oven and uncover. Sprinkle the cheese across the top of the casserole and transfer the uncovered skillet back into the oven for an additional 10 minutes, or until the cheese has completely melted.

Allow the casserole to rest out of the oven for 15 minutes. Serve directly to bowls with guacamole and sour cream.

“Imperial” Chicken and Rice
(Arroz Imperiál)
CUBA

TOTAL TIME: 1 hour, 30 minutes
CHARACTER: One Pot Meal
VESSEL: 9 x 13 inch baking dish, or equivalent
SERVES: 8-10

When we were in college, Greg and I met our buddy Ray Hechavarria. Ray is Cuban and he once got bonked on the head by a falling coconut. He’s fine. One day, I was invited to his home and his mom cooked for us. His mother is a terrific cook. *Arroz con pollo,* chicken and rice—a simple, delicious stalwart of Latino cuisine. Many years later, I learned of “Imperial” chicken and rice, which basically takes *arroz con pollo* and bonks it on the head with a coconut. This dish is incredibly crazy but undeniably delicious.

—Howie

RICE:

3¼ cups chicken broth

1 tsp turmeric powder (optional for yellow coloring)

1 tsp salt

2 cups jasmine or other long grain white rice, uncooked

CASSEROLE:

10 Tbsp mayonnaise, divided

6 oz ham, thin slices

12 oz Muenster cheese, thin slices

1 large red bell pepper, roasted, peeled, thin strips

¾ cup green olives, pitted

2 limes, cut into wedges

CHICKEN FILLING:

1½ - 2 lb chicken breasts, skinless, boneless

3 Tbsp extra-virgin olive oil, divided

1½ tsp salt, divided

1 tsp paprika

1 large onion, diced

1 large green bell pepper, diced

2 cloves garlic, minced

3 Tbsp tomato paste

½ cup dry white wine

¾ cup green peas, canned, drained or frozen, thawed

1 tsp ground black pepper

continued on page 98

Preheat the oven to 400°F.

In a medium pot on the stove, bring the broth, turmeric (if using), 1 teaspoon of salt, and rice to a boil. Reduce the heat to low, cover the pot and simmer for 20-25 minutes or until the rice has absorbed all the liquid.

To make the filling, in a small mixing bowl, coat the chicken with 1 tablespoon of olive oil, 1 teaspoon of salt, and paprika. Massage the chicken to spread seasonings evenly. Transfer the chicken to a sheet pan and roast in the oven for 25 minutes.

While the rice and chicken cook, place a skillet over medium-high heat. Add 1 tablespoon of olive oil. When the oil begins to shimmer, add the onion and pepper with the remaining ½ teaspoon of salt. Sauté for 6-8 minutes, or until the onion edges begin to brown. Add the garlic and tomato paste and continue to sauté for 3 minutes. Add the wine and allow it to reduce completely, about another 5-7 minutes. Stir in green peas and black pepper. Turn off the heat.

Remove the chicken from the oven, and shred with two forks, clean hands, or in a stand mixer with the paddle attachment. Stir the chicken into the cooling skillet mixture.

Lower the oven to 350°F.

To assemble the casserole, coat the bottom and sides of a baking dish with the remaining 1 tablespoon of olive oil. Layer half of the cooked rice in the bottom of the baking dish; flatten and compress with the back of a spoon or spatula. Smear 5 tablespoons of mayonnaise evenly atop the rice. Place the chicken mixture atop the mayonnaise, followed by a layer using half of the Muenster cheese and half of the roasted red peppers. Then, form another layer using the second half of the rice, the remaining mayonnaise, a layer of ham slices, and finally a layer of Muenster.

Transfer the baking dish to the oven and bake for 25-30 minutes, or until the cheese has melted and has barely begun to brown. Remove the casserole from the oven, garnish with roasted peppers and green olives, and serve hot. Squeeze of lime juice? Sure.

Plantain and Cheese Casserole
(Pastelón de Plántanos Maduros)

DOMINICAN REPUBLIC

TOTAL TIME: 1 hour, 15 minutes
CHARACTER: One Pot Meal, Main, Side
VESSEL: 9 x 13 inch baking dish, or equivalent
SERVES: 6-8

4 qt water
8 ripe plantains (primarily black skin), ends trimmed, halved widthwise
5 Tbsp extra-virgin olive oil, divided
1 large white onion, diced
1 large green bell pepper, diced
1 lb ground beef
1 tsp ground black pepper
1 tsp ground cumin
1 Tbsp adobo seasoning or chile powder
3 cloves garlic, minced
½ bunch cilantro, leaves chopped, stems minced
2 tsp salt, divided
½ cup raisins
½ cup green olives, pitted, halved
2 tsp dried oregano
1 14-oz can crushed tomatoes
½ cup dry white wine
1 Tbsp white vinegar
1½ cups white cheddar cheese, shredded
1½ cups Parmesan cheese, shredded
2 eggs, beaten

Plantains may look like bananas, but they are definitely *not bananas*. That said, there is colorful folklore in the Dominican Republic that claims that plantains *make* you bananas. Though plantains in general and this dish in particular are adored across the Republic, hungry citizens chow down on the stuff like it's going out of style, despite the risk of going crazy. So, we invite you to ascertain the validity of such folklore. Go bananas, which, of course are not plantains.

—Howie

continued on page 103

Preheat the oven to 375°F.

Place water and plantains in a large pot on the stove. Bring the water to a high simmer and let the plantains cook for 15 minutes. Remove the plantains from the water, drain, and set aside to cool.

While the plantains cook, start the filling by placing a skillet over medium heat. Add 1 tablespoon of olive oil. When the oil begins to shimmer, add onion and pepper to the skillet and sauté for 6-8 minutes, or until the onion becomes translucent. Add beef, black pepper, cumin, adobo or chile powder, garlic, cilantro stems, and 1 teaspoon of salt to the skillet and continue to sauté for 4-5 minutes, or until the beef is browned and broken into small pieces.

Add raisins, olives, oregano, tomato, wine, and vinegar to the skillet, bring the liquid to a boil, and reduce the heat to medium-low. Simmer the filling for 15 minutes, or until most of the liquid has evaporated.

When the plantains have cooled a bit, peel them and place in large mixing bowl. Add 3 tablespoons of olive oil, 1 remaining teaspoon of salt, and mash the plantains to a smooth consistency. In another mixing bowl, combine the cheeses.

To assemble the casserole, coat the bottom and sides of a baking dish with the remaining 1 tablespoon of olive oil. Spread half of the plantains in the bottom of the baking dish, flatten and compress with the back of a spoon or spatula. Place half of the cheese mixture atop the plantains, followed by the ground beef mixture, then the remaining half of the plantains. Smooth out the top. Pour the beaten eggs on top of the plantains, followed by the remaining half of the cheese mixture.

Transfer the baking dish to the oven and bake for 20-25 minutes or until the cheese on top has melted and begun to brown. Remove the pastelón from the oven and allow it to cool for 10 minutes before garnishing with cilantro leaves and serving heaping, gooey slices!

Tomato Tamale Pie
(Cazuela de Tamal)

MEXICO

TOTAL TIME: 1 hour, 40 minutes
CHARACTER: One Pot Meal, Main, Side
VESSEL: 9 x 13 inch baking dish, or equivalent
SERVES: 6–8

Back in 1993, Greg and I took our first road trip together from Santa Barbara to Las Vegas and the Grand Canyon! I had only just begun to appreciate the cuisines of the Southwest, having been raised in New York and New Jersey. To repair me, we took every opportunity to stop at a roadside stand in the desert and try whatever was on offer. Tamales altered my universe in profound ways. I truly appreciated the fine detail that went into crafting each scrumptious little steamed husk packet of corn meal and savory goop. That's a whole lot of work. This is much easier.

—Howie

FILLING:

8-10 medium (about 1½ -2 lb) Roma tomatoes, diced
2 tsp salt, divided
1 Tbsp extra-virgin olive oil
1 medium onion, diced
1 tsp black pepper
1 tsp ground cumin
½ tsp dry red pepper flakes
2 Tbsp all-purpose flour
1 clove garlic, minced
2 Tbsp tomato paste
½ cup dry white wine
2 sun-dried tomatoes, minced
1 4-oz can green chiles, diced
1 28-oz can diced tomatoes, drained

TOPPING:

2 cups yellow cornmeal
½ tsp salt
2 tsp baking powder
⅓ cup extra-virgin olive oil
Vegetable stock or water as needed

Preheat the oven to 400°F. In a colander over the sink or a large bowl, toss the fresh diced tomatoes with 1 teaspoon of salt. Let the tomatoes drain for at least 30 minutes while you prepare the other ingredients.

Place a skillet over medium heat. Add the olive oil. When the oil begins to shimmer, add the onion, spices, and remaining salt. Sauté until the onion begins to turn translucent, about 6–8 minutes. Sprinkle flour over the mixture, stir in, and continue to sauté for an additional minute.

Stir in garlic, tomato paste, wine, chiles, sun-dried tomatoes, and canned tomatoes. Allow this mixture to stew for 10 minutes. Transfer into a baking dish, smooth with a spoon, and top with the drained fresh tomatoes and let it cool for 15 minutes while you make the topping batter.

In a large mixing bowl, mix together cornmeal, salt, baking powder, and olive oil. Slowly add stock or water until a loose dough is formed. You're looking for the texture of creamy mashed potatoes.

Carefully spread the dough on top of mixture in the baking dish. Be careful that the dough sits on top of the fresh tomatoes and goes all the way to edges of the baking dish. Place the baking dish in the oven and bake for 30–35 minutes or until the cornbread topping begins to crack slightly.

Remove the tamale pie from the oven and allow to cool for 15 minutes before serving in bowls.

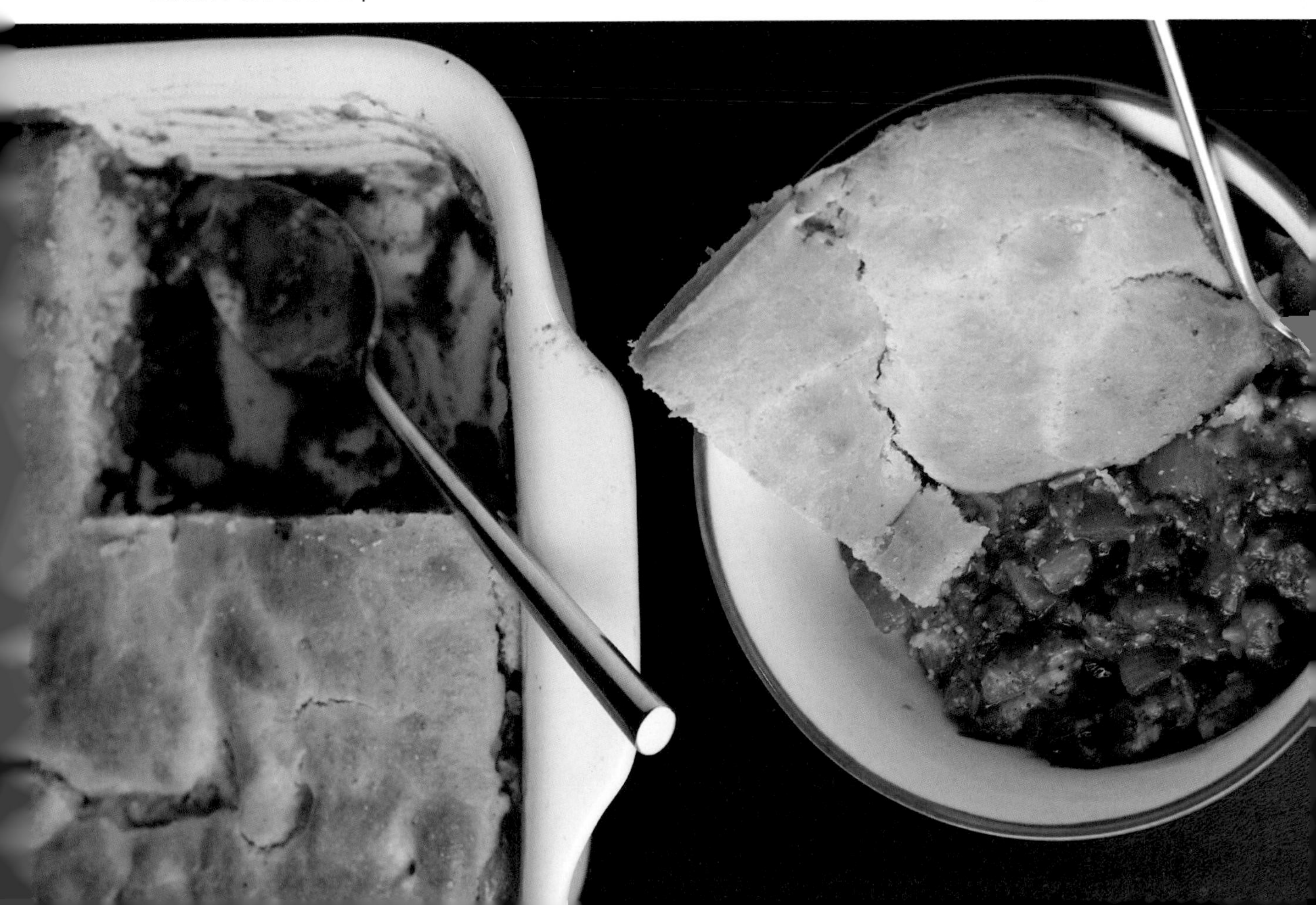

Meat and Bean Casserole
(Feijoada)
BRAZIL

TOTAL TIME: 4 hours, 30 minutes
CHARACTER: Main
VESSEL: 11 x 15 baking dish, or equivalent
SERVES: 10-12

Not unlike that famous French countryside favorite, *cassoulet, feijoada* was born of the need to use the whole animal. Of course, like many a dish that sprang from an impoverished class, it uses the cheaper, lower cuts of meat, while those cuts "high on the hog" went to the elite. Ah, you learned something there, *didn't you*? As I was saying, those elite, they have no idea what they were missing. The unctuous delicacy of melty, tender meat, the dreamy creaminess of the humble black bean, all together in a symphony of *not-being-rich*, yet much better fed.

—Greg

4 cups water
3 Tbsp extra-virgin olive oil
8 oz slab bacon, diced
1 large white onion, diced
1 bunch parsley, roughly chopped
2 tsp black pepper
12 oz pork shoulder, cut into 2-inch chunks
10 oz beef short rib, cut into 2-inch chunks
10 oz raw pork sausage links (spicy if you wish)
3 cloves garlic, minced
2 15-oz cans black beans, drained, rinsed
1 tsp salt
2 Tbsp soy sauce

Preheat the oven to 300°F. Bring the water to a boil in a kettle or pot, then drop the heat to maintain a simmer while you work.

Add olive oil to a separate skillet and heat over medium. When the oil begins to shimmer, sauté the bacon until it begins to brown, about 4 minutes. Add the onion, parsley, and black pepper, and sauté until the onion is translucent, about 6-8 minutes.

Transfer skillet contents to a baking dish. Add pork, beef, sausage, garlic, and simmering water to the baking dish. Stir to distribute the skillet contents evenly. Tightly seal the top of the baking dish with aluminum foil, and transfer to the oven for 2 hours.

Remove the baking dish from the oven, and carefully remove the foil. Add the beans, salt, and soy sauce to the skillet, distribute evenly, and place the baking dish back in the oven, uncovered, for an additional 2 hours. Stir the mixture occasionally. If it gets too dry, add water ½ cup at a time. The final texture should be creamy.

Remove the baking dish from oven. Serve along with steamed white rice and sautéed greens, such as spinach, kale, or Swiss chard.

Buttery Butternut Squash Casserole (Budín de Zapallos)

CHILE

TOTAL TIME: 2 hours, 15 minutes
CHARACTER: Side
VESSEL: 8 x 8 inch baking dish, or equivalent
SERVES: 6–8

1 large butternut squash or medium pumpkin
1 Tbsp extra-virgin olive oil
1 large onion, diced
1 tsp salt, divided
1 green bell pepper, seeded, roasted, peeled, diced
1 red bell pepper, seeded, roasted, peeled, diced
1 yellow bell pepper, seeded, roasted, peeled, diced
2 cloves garlic, minced
1 tsp ground cumin
1 tsp ancho or other chile powder
4 eggs, beaten
¼ cup heavy cream
2 Tbsp butter, melted
2 cups sharp cheddar cheese, shredded, divided

Have you ever traveled in the American Midwest and gone to a county fair boasting the "World's Largest Pumpkin" competition? Orange squash the size of tiny houses. *That'd make one hell of a jack-o-lantern!* Apparently, American exceptionalism knows no limits. In Chile, they have a more reasonable attitude. They actually grow their winter squash to eat them! It's a staple starch, like potatoes, rice, or pasta. Here, we offer a common dish that tastes nothing like a tiny house.

—Howie

Preheat the oven to 375°F.

Cut the squash or pumpkin in half lengthwise (tip to stem), scoop out the seeds, and place on a sheet pan with the cut sides facing downward. Roast in the oven for 45-50 minutes or until it is soft to the touch. Remove the squash from the oven and allow it to rest until it is cool enough to handle. Reduce the heat of the oven to 350°F.

While the squash is cooling, add olive oil to a skillet and heat over medium-low. When the oil begins to shimmer, add onion and ½ teaspoon of salt, and sauté until the onion is lightly caramelized, about 12-15 minutes.

Scoop the squash flesh from the skin and in a large mixing bowl, mash it with a fork or potato masher until smooth. To the mixing bowl, add the caramelized onions, roasted peppers, garlic, cumin, chile powder, eggs, cream, and butter. Mix thoroughly. Fold in 1 cup of shredded cheese. Transfer the mixing bowl contents to a baking dish and top with the remaining 1 cup of shredded cheese.

Cover the baking dish tightly with aluminum foil. Transfer the baking dish to the oven and bake for 20 minutes. Carefully remove the cover from the baking dish and continue to bake for an additional 35-40 minutes or until the center is no longer jiggly. Remove the casserole from the oven.

Serve warm scoops directly from the baking dish or wait for the casserole to cool to room temperature for full flavor.

Africa and The Middle East

Spicy Meatballs in Tomato Sauce
(Kefta Tagine)
MOROCCO

TOTAL TIME: 1 hour, 15 minutes
CHARACTER: Main
VESSEL: Moroccan tagine, 8 x 8 inch baking dish, or equivalent
SERVES: 3-5

> If you live near a Moroccan restaurant, you should go frequently. The aroma, the decor, the feast for both the taste buds and the eyes, and the . . . belly dancers? Beware, you may be rustled out of your seat by one of these exquisite creatures, and invited to do unspeakable, bumbling acts in front of otherwise satisfied diners, and of course your adoring friends who shamed you into getting up in the first place! Forgive me for getting personal. Allow me to distract you with this dish that will undoubtedly be waiting at your table when you return from your brief career as a belly dancer.
>
> —Howie

SAUCE:
1 Tbsp extra-virgin olive oil
1 onion, diced
1 tsp salt
1 jalapeño pepper, minced
1 28-oz can crushed or pureed tomatoes
2 Tbsp tomato paste
2 tsp hot or other paprika
1 tsp cumin
¼ tsp ground black pepper

MEATBALLS:
1 lb ground beef
½ onion, grated or finely diced
3 Tbsp parsley, roughly chopped
3 Tbsp cilantro, roughly chopped
1 tsp salt
½ tsp ground black pepper
1 tsp cumin
1 tsp ground cinnamon
2 tsp hot or other paprika
½ tsp cayenne pepper

To make the sauce, place a skillet over medium heat. Add olive oil. When the oil begins to shimmer, add onion and salt and sauté 4-6 minutes, or until translucent. Add the jalapeño pepper and sauté another 2-3 minutes. Add remaining sauce ingredients. Lower to a simmer, and let it cook, uncovered, while you prepare your meatballs—10-30 minutes. The longer you simmer the sauce, the better it will taste.

Heat the oven to 350°F. To make the meatballs, in a large mixing bowl, thoroughly combine all ingredients. Form the mixture into 1½-inch balls, about 15-18 in this recipe.

Transfer the sauce into a tagine or baking dish. Place meatballs into the sauce. Cover the vessel with a lid or tightly with aluminum foil, and transfer to the oven and braise for 25-30 minutes, or until the meatballs are just cooked through.

Remove the saucy kefta from the oven, uncover, and sprinkle additional parsley and/or cilantro across the top. Serve immediately over couscous, atop rice, or with warm, crusty bread.

Flaky Cinnamon-Almond Chicken Pie
(Bastilla)
MOROCCO

TOTAL TIME: 1 hour, 40 minutes
CHARACTER: Main
VESSEL: 9 x 9 inch baking dish, or equivalent
SERVES: 3-4

1 sheet puff pastry
2 cups water
½ tsp salt
½ tsp ground ginger
½ tsp ground cumin
3 tsp ground cinnamon, divided
1 pinch of saffron (optional)
1 lb chicken breast fillets or thighs, boneless, skinless
½ cup sliced almonds
3 Tbsp sugar
3 large eggs
1 Tbsp lemon juice (about ½ a lemon)
2 Tbsp butter, melted, divided
Powdered sugar for garnish

When Howie and I went to our first Moroccan restaurant, the first surprise was the belly dancer. Our enthusiastic response probably led to the second surprise, which was our joining the belly dancer. The third surprise? Well, let's just say that perhaps I showed a bit too much of my belly than was entirely appropriate. But the fourth surprise—it was the best of all. When a crispy phyllo package was delivered to our table, and we opened it to discover the bastilla. Who could imagine that chicken, cinnamon, and a touch of sugar would be even more entrancing than a belly dancer?

—Greg

Preheat the oven to 375°F. Remove the puff pastry from the freezer and allow to thaw for about 30 minutes on the counter, per the package's instructions.

In a medium pot on the stove, combine water, salt, ginger, cumin, 1 teaspoon of cinnamon, and (optionally) saffron. Over medium heat, bring the mixture to a boil. Lower the heat to a simmer and add the chicken. Poach the chicken until cooked through, about 25-30 minutes.

While the chicken is poaching, add the almonds to a baking dish, and place in the oven to roast for 8-10 minutes, or until the almonds begin to toast and start to turn light blond in color. Remove

continued on page 116

the toasted almonds to a bowl and combine with the sugar and the remaining 2 teaspoons of cinnamon.

When the chicken is cooked, remove it to a bowl, leaving the broth in the pot. Turn the heat to medium and allow the broth to reduce until you have about ½ cup remaining, about 10-15 minutes. While the broth is reducing, use two forks to shred the cooked chicken. Combine the chicken with the almond and sugar mixture, mixing to coat the chicken well.

In a small mixing bowl, beat the eggs until frothy. Once the chicken broth has reduced, add the lemon juice to the pot. Next, stir in the eggs. Continue to stir regularly, cooking the eggs and continuing to reduce the broth until the pot has the consistency of scrambled eggs—about 8-10 minutes. Remove the eggs from heat.

Dust your counter or board with flour, unfold the puff pastry, place the sheet atop the flour, and dust with some more flour. Roll the sheet into a 10-inch square, smoothing out all the fold seams.

Using a pastry brush, generously coat the bottom of the empty baking dish with half of the melted butter. Layer the shredded chicken and almonds, then the eggs. Top with the sheet of puff pastry, pushing down to tightly fit the filling. Trim the excess pastry from the edges. Generously brush the puff pastry with the remaining butter, and place the baking dish in the oven.

Bake for 25 minutes, or until the pastry is lightly brown. Sprinkle powdered sugar over the pastry. Allow to cool for about 10 minutes and serve in heaping spoonfuls.

Chicken and Lentil Casserole
(Doro Wat)
ETHIOPIA

TOTAL TIME: 2 hours
CHARACTER: Main
VESSEL: 9 x 13 inch baking dish, or equivalent
SERVES: 4–6

In Washington, DC, we have an embarrassment of international dining riches. Many years ago, I went to an elaborate work dinner at one of the best Ethiopian joints in town. We had a wide array of colorful dishes served atop a huge and unique sourdough flatbread, of course all served communally. A small tear of bread and a pinch of this, another tear and a pinch of that. I became obsessed with a small tear of bread with this and that *together*. Where "doro wat," or stewed chicken is traditionally a stand-alone dish, I favored it paired with some similarly flavored lentils. Here is an adaptation of my favorite bite.

—Howie

1 cup lentils
1 tsp garlic powder
4 Tbsp berbere or hot chile powder, divided
1½ tsp salt, divided
3 cups water, boiling
2 large red onions, diced or minced
⅓ cup nit'r kibe, clarified butter or unsalted butter
2 Tbsp tomato paste
2 cloves garlic, minced
1 Tbsp ginger, minced
½ cup dry red wine
1 cup chicken broth
2 lb chicken thighs, bone-in, skin removed
2 limes, juiced

Preheat the oven to 350°F.

In a baking dish, combine lentils, garlic powder, 1 tablespoon of berbere or chile powder, ½ teaspoon of salt, and 3 cups of boiling water. Cover tightly with aluminum foil and transfer the baking dish to the oven. Cook for 50-55 minutes, or until the lentils have absorbed the water.

While the lentils are cooking, make the onion sauce. Place a skillet over medium heat and add the onions and 1 teaspoon of salt. Sauté the onions for 15-20 minutes or until the onions are very soft and have begun to caramelize. Add nit'r kibe or butter, tomato paste, garlic, ginger, and the

continued on page 119

remaining 3 tablespoons of berbere or chile powder to the skillet and continue to sauté for an additional 20 minutes, or until the onions have turned a deep reddish brown and begun to break down into a paste.

Add wine to the skillet and simmer for 10 minutes, or until the wine reduces by more than half. Add broth and continue to simmer for 10 minutes.

Remove the lentils from the oven and carefully remove the foil. Stir the lentils to ensure the spices are distributed, and create a flat layer. Smear half of the onion sauce atop the lentils. Place chicken thighs atop the onion sauce, and smear the top of the chicken evenly with the remainder of the onion sauce.

Return the baking dish to the oven and roast, uncovered, for 50-55 minutes. Remove the doro wat from the oven and squeeze lime juice on top. Serve pieces of chicken and some lentils and be sure to include plenty of onion sauce. Traditionally, it is served with fresh injera (Ethiopian pancake) or rice.

Spicy Red Rice (Jollof)

GHANA

TOTAL TIME: 1 hour, 20 minutes
CHARACTER: Side
VESSEL: 9 x 13 inch baking dish, or equivalent
SERVES: 6-8

> Wouldn't we all be happier if we had more J-words in our life? Jolly, jiggle, juggle, jump, jumble, jazzy! Don't they just make you smile? Heck, even *justice* starts with a J! Anyway, this dish is called jollof, so I endorse it! Jollof makes me jubilant!
>
> —Greg

- 3 small tomatoes, quartered
- 1 large red bell pepper, stemmed, seeded, split apart
- 1 habañero pepper, stemmed, seeded
- 3 Tbsp extra-virgin olive oil
- 1 large onion, diced
- 1 large carrot, diced
- 1 tsp cumin
- 1 tsp garlic powder
- 1 tsp turmeric
- 1 tsp berbere or other chile powder
- 1 tsp salt
- 3 Tbsp tomato paste
- 1 lb frozen okra, thawed, sliced
- 1 jalapeño pepper, stemmed, seeded, diced
- 2 cups vegetable broth
- 2 cups jasmine or other long grain white rice, uncooked

Preheat the oven to 375°F. In a blender, puree tomatoes, bell pepper, and habañero. Set aside.

Place a skillet over medium heat and add the olive oil. When the oil begins to shimmer, add the onion, carrot, cumin, garlic powder, turmeric, berbere, and salt, and sauté until the onion becomes almost translucent, about 6-8 minutes. Add tomato paste and continue to sauté for 3 minutes.

Add the blender purée to the skillet, along with okra and jalapeño. Reduce the heat to medium-low and allow the mixture to simmer for 10 minutes. Add broth and bring back to a simmer.

Place rice in a baking dish. Pour skillet contents over the rice, stirring to combine. Cover tightly with aluminum foil and bake in the oven for 35 minutes.

Remove the jollof from the oven and allow it to rest, covered, for 15 minutes. Remove the foil, fluff, and serve directly to bowls. It's popular across Western Africa to serve jollof as an accompaniment to meat or fish.

Fruity Curried Meat Casserole
(Bobotie)
SOUTH AFRICA

TOTAL TIME: 1 hour, 30 minutes
CHARACTER: Main
VESSEL: 9 x 13 inch baking dish, or equivalent
SERVES: 6-8

This is the national dish of South Africa. It makes sense. It truly is a sum of trade, immigration, and native culinary attitudes. The Italians of the mid-17th century were huge fans of grinding lower cuts of meat and incorporating the flavors that were being sailed in from the trading routes across the Mediterranean, all thanks to the Dutch East India Company. Hollanders then layered it with a favorite Euro-custard and brought it down to Cape Town. Finally, the South Africans thought it only natural to throw in what they absorbed directly from the Arab states in the form of fruit and spices. *Bam*. Actual fusion cuisine.

—Howie

FILLING:

2 Tbsp extra-virgin olive oil, divided
1 large onion, diced
1 large apple, peeled, cored, diced
4 slices bread (about 5 oz)
¼ cup water
2 lb ground beef or lamb
1 egg, beaten
½ cup raisins
3 Tbsp peach jam
1 Tbsp ginger, grated or minced
1 lemon, juiced
2 tsp salt
1 tsp ground black pepper
1 tsp smoked paprika
2 tsp turmeric
1 tsp ground cumin seeds
1 tsp dried thyme
1 tsp ground cinnamon

CUSTARD TOPPING:

3 eggs
2 cups milk
½ tsp salt
½ tsp ground black pepper
½ tsp dried thyme
Greek-style yogurt for garnish

continued on page 124

Preheat the oven to 350°F.

Place a skillet over medium heat. Add 1 tablespoon of olive oil. When the oil begins to shimmer, sauté the onion and apple until the onion is translucent, about 6-8 minutes.

To make the filling, place bread chunks in a large mixing bowl. Slowly pour water over the bread chunks until all of the bread is moistened. Using clean hands, mash the bread until it forms a paste, being sure to only use as much water as needed to form a paste. To the mixing bowl, add onion and apple from the skillet, ground meat, and the remaining filling ingredients. Blend until mixed evenly.

Coat the bottom and sides of a baking dish with the remaining 1 tablespoon of olive oil. Scrape the filling from the mixing bowl to the baking dish. Cover the baking dish tightly with aluminum foil and transfer to the oven and bake for 30-35 minutes, or until the meat mixture has shrunken slightly. Remove the baking dish from the oven.

Carefully pour any loose liquids and oils from the baking dish. Using the back of a spoon or spatula, press the meat back to the edges of the baking dish in a flat layer.

In a mixing bowl, whisk together the custard ingredients (except the yogurt) and pour over the meat. Return the uncovered baking dish to the oven and continue to bake for an additional 40-45 minutes, or until the top begins to brown.

Allow the casserole to cool for 15 minutes before slicing and serving beautiful blocks with a dollop of yogurt and some rice!

Chickpea Eggplant and Pita Casserole

(Fateh al Badhinjan)

JORDAN

TOTAL TIME: 1 hour, 30 minutes
CHARACTER: Main, Side
VESSEL: 8 x 8 inch baking dish, or equivalent
SERVES: 4–6

> Three words: Middle Eastern nachos. Okay, five words: Rich, lemony, Middle Eastern nachos. Not quite. How about eight words? Rich, creamy, crunchy, lemony, spicy, Middle Eastern nachos. Close. Fourteen words: Rich, creamy, crunchy, lemony, spicy, Middle Eastern nachos that you must eat right now. Yeah, that's it.
>
> —Greg

EGGPLANT:

2 medium eggplants, peeled, diced
3 Tbsp extra-virgin olive oil
½ tsp salt

CASSEROLE:

4 pieces of pita bread, torn into bite-sized pieces
1 Tbsp extra-virgin olive oil
1 15-oz can chickpeas, drained and rinsed
½ cup tahini
½ tsp salt
Juice of 1 lemon
¼ cup water
¼ cup parsley, roughly chopped
3 Tbsp pine nuts, toasted

TOMATO SAUCE:

1 Tbsp extra-virgin olive oil
1 large onion, diced
1 green bell pepper, diced
1 tsp salt
3 cloves garlic, minced
½ tsp ground cinnamon
½ tsp ground allspice
¼ tsp ground coriander
¼ tsp dried red pepper flakes (optional)
1 15-oz can pureed tomatoes
2 Tbsp tomato paste

continued on page 127

Preheat oven to 450°F.

In a large mixing bowl, combine the eggplant, olive oil, and salt. Toss the eggplant to coat. Place the eggplant on a sheet pan in a single layer. Transfer the sheet pan to the oven and roast for 15-20 minutes, or until the eggplant is soft and beginning to brown. Remove the eggplant from the oven and set the oven to low broil.

While the eggplant is roasting, make tomato sauce by placing a skillet over medium-high heat. Add olive oil. When the oil begins to shimmer, add the onion, green pepper, and salt. Sauté until the onion begins to turn translucent, about 6-8 minutes. Add the garlic, cinnamon, allspice, coriander, and red pepper flakes (if using) and sauté until fragrant, about 30 seconds. Stir in the tomatoes and tomato paste. Lower the heat to a simmer and allow the sauce to cook for at least 20 minutes.

While the sauce is simmering, in a large mixing bowl, toss the pita pieces with olive oil. Place the pita on a sheet pan and toast in the oven, about 3-5 minutes. Remove the pita from the oven and set aside.

Warm the chickpeas in the microwave for 2 minutes, or in a pot of boiling water on the stove for 5 minutes. Drain and reserve. In a small mixing bowl, whisk together the tahini, salt, lemon juice, and water.

To assemble the fateh, in a baking dish atop the toasted pita, layer the roasted eggplant, then the tomato sauce, then the chickpeas. Finish by pouring the tahini sauce across the top. Place the fateh under a low broiler for about 1 minute, or until the sauce begins to firm up and brown. Remove and garnish with parsley and toasted pine nuts.

Serve in scoops that include all the tasty parts!

Ginger-Clove Pilaf

(Pilau)

TANZANIA

TOTAL TIME: 1 hour, 20 minutes
CHARACTER: One Pot Meal, Main
VESSEL: 8 x 8 inch baking dish, or equivalent
SERVES: 4-6

I once went on a trip to Tanzania. It was awesome. Apart from the shock of watching the *circle of life*—up close—on safari, my second biggest surprise was the food. It left an indelible mark on my culinary attitudes toward Africa. Though most of my time was on the mainland, it was my visit to the island of Zanzibar that sent me for a loop. It was essentially eating the Middle East due to a history as a trade hub for Arab goods, read: SPICES. This pilaf dish, to me, is Zanzibar on a plate.

—Howie

3½ cups chicken broth
2 Tbsp extra-virgin olive oil
1 lb chicken thighs, boneless, skinless, diced
2 cups basmati or other long grain white rice, uncooked
1 large onion, diced
1 tsp salt
½ green bell pepper, diced
3 cloves garlic, minced
1 Tbsp ginger, minced
6 whole cloves
1 cinnamon stick
½ tsp ground cumin
½ tsp ground black pepper
¼ tsp ground cardamom
¼ tsp turmeric powder
2 Tbsp tomato paste

Preheat oven to 375°F. In a small pot, bring chicken broth to a simmer and leave on low.

Place a large skillet over medium heat and add the olive oil. When the oil begins to shimmer, add the chicken and sauté for 4-6 minutes, until the chicken has browned. Add the rice, onion, salt, and green bell pepper, and sauté until the rice begins to toast and the onion becomes almost translucent, about 6-8 minutes. Add garlic and ginger and continue to sauté until fragrant, about 1 minute.

Add remaining ingredients. Stir well, and cook for another minute. Remove from heat. Carefully pour the skillet contents into a baking dish and add the hot chicken broth. Cover the baking dish tightly with aluminum foil and transfer to the oven for 55 minutes.

Remove the pilau from the oven and allow to rest, covered, for 15 minutes. Uncover; fish out and remove the cinnamon stick before serving steaming scoops.

Upside Down Cauliflower Rice
(Maqluba)
JORDAN

TOTAL TIME: 1 hour, 30 minutes
CHARACTER: One Pot Meal, Main
VESSEL: 8 x 8 inch baking dish, or equivalent
SERVES: 4-6

I have to be honest. About half the time I make this dish, it doesn't come out of the pot quite like it did when I took the picture. Maybe the rice is a bit sticky, or maybe the whole tower sorta crumbles. But you know what? It doesn't matter one iota. The taste on this one is sublime. So relax and enjoy, no matter how it turns out . . . Or, hold the photo up for your guests!

—Greg

½ head cauliflower, cut into small florets
2 tsp extra-virgin olive oil
½ tsp paprika
1½ tsp salt, divided
½ tsp ground black pepper, divided
3 Tbsp butter, divided
2 small onions, diced (about 2 cups)
1 lb chicken thighs, boneless, skinless, diced
3 cloves garlic, crushed
1 tsp ground cumin
½ tsp ground cinnamon
½ tsp allspice
4 carrots, peeled and shredded (about 1 cup)
2 cups basmati or other long grain rice, uncooked
3 cups chicken broth
¼ tsp turmeric
¼ cup pine nuts

Preheat the oven to 425°F.

In a large mixing bowl, combine the cauliflower, olive oil, paprika, ½ teaspoon of salt, and ¼ teaspoon of the black pepper. Toss the cauliflower to coat. Line a sheet pan with parchment paper and place the cauliflower in a single layer. Transfer the sheet pan to the oven and roast for 20-25 minutes, or until the cauliflower is golden brown.

While the cauliflower is roasting, place a large skillet over medium heat and add 2 tablespoons of butter. When the butter begins to bubble, add the onions and sauté until they become almost

continued on page 132

translucent, about 6-8 minutes. Add the chicken and continue to sauté for 4-6 minutes, or until well-browned. Add the garlic, cumin, cinnamon, allspice, the remaining salt and pepper, and cook until fragrant, about 1 minute. Remove the skillet from the heat.

Remove the cauliflower from the oven and reduce the temperature to 350°F.

Using the 1 remaining tablespoon of butter, coat the insides of a baking dish. Layer the chicken along the bottom. Next, layer in the cauliflower. Next, layer the carrots. Top with an even layer of rice.

Mix the turmeric into the chicken broth and slowly pour it into the baking dish, being sure not to disturb the layers. Cover the baking dish tightly with aluminum foil and transfer to the oven for 35-40 minutes, or until the rice is fully cooked.

While the maqluba is in the oven, place a dry skillet over medium heat. Add the pine nuts. Cook for 3-4 minutes, stirring often, until the nuts are fragrant and slightly browned. Keep a close eye on them, as they go from uncooked to burned very quickly!

Remove the maqluba from the oven. To serve, run a knife around the edges of the maqluba. Place a large platter over the top of the baking dish, and carefully flip. You may need to lightly jiggle and tap the baking dish in order to get the maqluba to release. If all else fails—just spoon it out. It won't be as pretty, but I promise, your taste buds will never know.

Persian Layered Chicken Rice
(Tahchin Morgh)
IRAN

TOTAL TIME: 2 hours, 20 minutes
CHARACTER: One Pot Meal, Main
VESSEL: 8 x 8 inch baking dish, or equivalent
SERVES: 4-6

1 onion, diced
1½ lb chicken thighs, skinless, boneless
½ tsp ground black pepper
1 tsp ground turmeric
1½ tsp salt, divided
4-5 cups water, divided
2 cups basmati or other long grain rice, uncooked
4 Tbsp butter, divided
½ tsp saffron threads
2 large eggs, beaten
1 cup Greek-style yogurt
3 Tbsp extra-virgin olive oil
1 lemon, sliced

> If this world has two hundred countries and five hundred cuisines, there must be over a thousand versions of chicken and rice, each better than the last. This version is delicious in its simplicity, with very little distraction from the nutty, aromatic basmati and falling-apart braised chicken. It is a bit of work to prepare, but gorgeous and worth every minute.
>
> —Greg

Place a pot over high heat. Add the onion, chicken, pepper, turmeric, 1 teaspoon of salt, and 2 cups of water. Once the water comes to a boil, lower heat to a simmer, cover tightly, and allow the chicken to stew for 40-45 minutes, or until the chicken is fully cooked and falling apart.

While the chicken is cooking, place a second pot over medium heat. Combine the rice with the remaining 2–3 cups of water, 2 tablespoons of butter, saffron threads, and the remaining ½ teaspoon of salt. Once it comes to a boil, turn down the heat to a light simmer. Stir to ensure that the butter has melted, cover, and allow the rice to cook until the water is gone, about 10 minutes. Turn off the heat; remove the lid and set aside. The rice should only be partially cooked.

Preheat oven to 400°F. Remove the chicken from the first pot. Roughly chop into bite-sized pieces and set aside.

continued on page 135

In a large mixing bowl, combine eggs, yogurt, and olive oil. Add the partially cooked rice and stir until all the rice is coated evenly.

Place the remaining 2 tablespoons of butter in a (preferably glass) baking dish and place in the oven. Allow the butter to completely melt and begin to bubble. Carefully remove the baking dish from the oven.

Spread half of the rice mixture evenly along the bottom. Next, form a layer using all the cooked chicken. Finally, top with an even layer using the remainder of the rice mixture. Cover the baking dish tightly with aluminum foil and return to the oven. Roast for 50-60 minutes, or until the bottom is golden brown.

Remove the baking dish from the oven. Uncover and run a flat, narrow spatula or a knife along the sides of the baking dish, to release the casserole. Place a large serving platter upside down, on top of the baking dish, and cautiously invert the whole thing in a single motion. Allow it to rest for 10-15 minutes before removing the baking dish from the upside-down casserole. Then, slice and serve with a slice of lemon.

Meatloaf with Lemon Tahini Sauce (Kofta bi Tahini)

LEBANON

TOTAL TIME: 1 hour, 20 minutes
CHARACTER: Main
VESSEL: 9 x 13 inch baking dish, or equivalent
SERVES: 4–6

I'll admit it. I've never ordered the meatloaf off a menu, though it's been recommended plenty. Those folks on Yelp always seem to love it. I love eating it at home. And yet, at a restaurant, I've never pulled the trigger. What is it about me, Dr. Freud, that prevents me from ordering the meatloaf? I'm telling you, Dr. Jung, I love myself! But, apparently, I can't love the meatloaf lover within. What does it mean? What can it mean? If only *this* dish were on a menu, I would no doubt save a ton on therapy.

—Greg

MEATLOAF:

1 cup parsley, diced finely
1 lb ground beef
1 onion, diced finely
1 tomato, diced finely
2 Tbsp extra-virgin olive oil
1 tsp salt
½ tsp allspice
½ tsp cinnamon

POTATO LAYER:

4 qt water
2 large potatoes (about 1 lb), cut into ¼ inch thick rounds

TAHINI SAUCE:

1 cup tahini
Juice of 3 lemons (about ⅓ cup)
½ tsp salt
2 cups water

Preheat oven to 425°F.

Reserve 2 tablespoons of parsley in a small bowl. In a large mixing bowl, combine beef, onion, tomato, olive oil, salt, allspice, cinnamon, and the remainder of the parsley. Using a large spoon (or a clean hand), stir until just combined.

continued on page 138

Spread the meat mixture evenly across the bottom of a baking dish. Use your finger to make 6 rows of 5 indentations, each about halfway through the meat. In the next step, this will allow the flavor of the sauce to penetrate the meat while cooking. Transfer the baking dish to the oven and roast for 20 minutes.

While the meat is cooking, in a large pot, bring water to a boil. Add the potato slices and boil for 5 minutes, until partially cooked. Drain the potatoes and reserve.

In a mixing bowl, whisk together tahini, lemon juice, salt, and water until smooth. The sauce will be very loose.

Remove the baking dish from the oven. Place the partially cooked potato slices on top of the meat in a single layer. There will be some overlap. Evenly pour the tahini sauce across the potatoes. Cover the baking dish tightly with foil, cutting a few slits in the foil to let steam escape. Return the baking dish to the oven for another 20 minutes.

Carefully remove the foil and roast for a final 20 minutes.

To finish, turn the oven to broil and allow the casserole to brown for 4-6 minutes, keeping a close eye on it. Remove the casserole from the oven, garnish with the reserved 2 tablespoons of parsley, and serve.

Bulgur Wheat and Meat Pie
(Kibbeh bil Sanieh)
SYRIA

TOTAL TIME: 2 hours, 25 minutes
CHARACTER: Main, Side
VESSEL: 9 x 13 inch baking dish, or equivalent
SERVES: 6-8

Kibbeh are middle-eastern version of corn dogs, only much, much better. Spiced ground meat, surrounded by a torpedo of sweetened bulgur wheat. Deep fried and served hot, no stick. This casserole gives you all of that flavor, with none of the fuss or the frying. I've brought it to many a potluck, but have yet to find anyone who doesn't go crazy for this dish.

—Greg

CRUST:

2 cups #2 fine-grain, or other bulgur wheat
2½ cups hot water
1 Tbsp salt
3 tsp canola or vegetable oil, divided
½ cup bread crumbs
½ cup all-purpose flour
1 Tbsp ground cumin
1 Tbsp paprika
1 Tbsp honey

FILLING:

½ cup pine nuts
1 medium onion, diced
1 tsp salt
2 cloves garlic, minced
1 lb ground lamb or beef
½ tsp ground cinnamon
½ tsp allspice
1 tsp paprika
½ tsp ground black pepper
1 tsp pomegranate molasses
Greek-style yogurt and mint for garnish

Preheat the oven to 350°F. To prepare your crust, place bulgur and hot water into a large mixing bowl. Allow to soak for 30 minutes until water is fully absorbed. Using hands or a wooden spoon, knead the salt and 1 teaspoon of oil into the bulgur for 2 minutes. Add bread crumbs, flour, cumin, paprika, and honey to the bulgur and knead for an additional 5 minutes. Cover and set aside for at least 30 minutes.

continued on page 141

To toast the pine nuts, place a dry skillet over medium heat. Add pine nuts. Cook for 3–5 minutes, occasionally stirring and keeping a very close eye on the nuts, as they will go from raw to burned very quickly. Remove from skillet when pine nuts are lightly toasted and fragrant.

To prepare the filling, place a skillet over medium high heat. Add 1 teaspoon of oil. When the oil begins to shimmer, add the onion and sauté for 4–6 minutes, until the onion pieces begin to brown at the edges. Add garlic and cook until fragrant, about 30 seconds. Add ground meat, breaking it up with a spatula until browned, about 6–8 minutes.

Move the meat to the edges of the skillet, leaving an open area in the middle. In that space, add the cinnamon, allspice, paprika, and pepper. Toast spices for 15–20 seconds, until fragrant. Then quickly stir to coat the onions and meat, and sauté for 1 minute. Stir in half of the toasted pine nuts, and the pomegranate molasses, and remove the skillet from the heat.

Coat the bottom and sides of a baking dish with 1 teaspoon of oil. Take half of the bulgur mixture and press into the bottom of the dish in one even layer. Spread beef mixture over the bottom crust and finish by spreading the last of the bulgur mixture evenly over the top of the meat. It helps to form thin patties of the crust with one's hands before placing atop the meat. Once you mostly cover the meat with bulgur crust, use a wet hand to smooth the top over and fill in any gaps.

To make the kibbeh more beautiful, use the top of a spoon or a knife to create decorative dents in the top crust. Place baking dish in oven and roast for 35-40 minutes, until crust is fully cooked and browned. Remove from oven. Allow the casserole to cool for 10 minutes, garnish with yogurt, mint, the remaining pine nuts, and serve in wedges or squares.

Cauliflower Yogurt Pot
(Zahra bi Laban)
LEBANON

TOTAL TIME: 1 hour, 30 minutes
CHARACTER: Main, Side
VESSEL: 8 x 8 inch baking dish, or equivalent
SERVES: 4-6

> Roasted cauliflower is plenty good on its own. But combined with a savory, spiced yogurt sauce? And then roasting them together into a burbling, bubbling pot of creaminess? You've got to be kidding me. I didn't know vegetables could do this!
>
> —Greg

1 head cauliflower, small florets
2 Tbsp extra-virgin olive oil
2 tsp salt, divided
2 cups beef broth
3 cups Greek-style yogurt
1 tsp paprika
1 tsp cumin
1 tsp garlic powder
½ tsp cinnamon
½ tsp ground black pepper
1 Tbsp cornstarch

Preheat oven to 425°F.

In a large mixing bowl, combine the cauliflower, olive oil, and 1 teaspoon of salt. Toss to coat. Line a sheet pan with parchment paper and place the cauliflower in a single layer. Transfer the sheet pan to the oven and roast for 20-25 minutes, or until the cauliflower is golden brown.

Remove from the oven and lower the temperature to 325°F. Transfer the cauliflower into a baking dish.

In a mixing bowl, whisk together the remaining ingredients. Pour this broth mixture over the cauliflower in the baking dish and stir to combine. Cover the baking dish tightly with aluminum foil or a lid, and roast in the oven for 30 minutes. Carefully remove the foil or lid and continue to roast for an additional 30 minutes.

Remove the casserole from the oven and serve hot scoops over rice or alongside the Persian Layered Chicken Rice from page 133.

Europe

Cheesy Fish Bake
(Ofnsteiktur Fiskur Með Lauk Og Osti)
ICELAND

TOTAL TIME: 45 minutes
CHARACTER: Main
VESSEL: 8 x 8 inch baking dish, or equivalent
SERVES: 6-8

- 1½ lb cod fillets, cut into 2-inch pieces
- 1 tsp salt, divided
- 1 lemon, grated, zest and juice divided
- 1½ cups cream
- 1 Tbsp Dijon mustard
- 1 tsp black pepper
- 3 Tbsp butter, melted, divided
- 1½ cups Emmenthaler or gruyere cheese, grated
- ½ cup bread crumbs

I feel like you hear this everywhere: *Cheese and fish don't go together!* Chefs across the globe look down on the pairing as an abomination and virtually toxic, without giving so much as an explanation. Of course, there are some notable exceptions: that classic tuna melt, anchovy pizza, shrimp and cheesy grits, blue cheese and mussels, lasagna al tonno, and lobster mac and cheese are among my favorites. But this, *this* is not nuanced. It is *fish and cheese in your face.* I dare you to tell me this combination doesn't work.

—Howie

Preheat the oven to 325°F.

In a mixing bowl, mix together the cod pieces, lemon juice, and ½ teaspoon of salt. Allow the cod to marinate while you prepare the other ingredients.

In a separate mixing bowl, whisk together cream, mustard, black pepper, and the remaining ½ teaspoon of salt. In a third mixing bowl, mix together 2 tablespoons of melted butter, lemon zest, cheese, and bread crumbs.

Using the remaining 1 tablespoon of butter, coat the bottom and sides of a baking dish. Place the cod pieces in the baking dish in an even layer. Pour the cream mixture over the cod, then evenly distribute the cheesy bread crumb mixture across the top. Transfer the baking dish to the oven and bake for 35-40 minutes, or until the top is golden brown.

Remove the casserole from the oven and serve warm scoops over leafy greens.

“Swedish” Sausage Potato Casserole

(Svensk Pølseret)

DENMARK

TOTAL TIME: 1 hour
CHARACTER: Main
VESSEL: 9 x 13 inch baking dish, or equivalent
SERVES: 6-8

2 (about 1 lb) russet potatoes, peeled, shredded, rinsed
2 Tbsp extra-virgin olive oil
1½ tsp salt, divided
4 Tbsp (½ stick) butter
1 large onion, diced
1 Tbsp smoked paprika
1 lb hot dogs (the fancier the better), cut into rounds
¼ cup flour
4 Tbsp tomato paste
2 cups milk
1 tsp ground black pepper
¼ cup parsley, roughly chopped

Have you ever wondered what would happen if your backyard barbecue hot dogs ever staged an escape attempt, leapt from the grill, took cover in a bowl of ketchup, then snuck their way to the picnic table where they accidentally stumbled into the tub of potato salad? Stop wondering and make this dish. Oh, and if you're asking yourself why this is called “Swedish” though it's from Denmark, you're in the same boat as most Danes.

—Howie

Preheat the oven to 375°F.

Squeeze-dry the potato shreds in a clean dish towel or paper towels. In a large mixing bowl, toss the potato shreds with olive oil and ½ teaspoon of salt. Spread the mixture loosely along the bottom of a baking dish. Cover the baking dish tightly with aluminum foil and transfer to the oven for 15-20 minutes, or until the potato shreds are just cooked.

As the potatoes cook, place a skillet over medium heat. Add butter. Once the butter melts, add onion and sauté the until nearly translucent, about 4-6 minutes. Add hot dogs and continue to sauté for another 5-7 minutes, or until the hot dogs have slightly browned. Sprinkle flour into the skillet and mix it into the onion and hot dogs. Stir in tomato paste and sauté this mixture for 2 minutes. Then slowly stir in the milk, making sure there are no clumps. Continue to stir the mixture until it comes to a boil. Turn off the heat and stir in black pepper and the remaining 1 teaspoon of salt.

Remove the potatoes from the oven and carefully remove the foil. Transfer skillet contents into the baking dish and mix it with the potatoes. Return the baking dish back to the oven and roast for an additional 20 minutes.

Remove the Pølseret from the oven and serve hot scoops immediately, sprinkled with parsley.

Smashed Rutabaga Pie
(Lanttu Laatikko)
FINLAND

TOTAL TIME: 1 hour, 45 minutes
CHARACTER: Side
VESSEL: 9 x 9 inch baking dish, or equivalent
SERVES: 6-8

Until my buddy Jim introduced me to Lanttu Laatikko, the only time I'd encountered the famed rutabaga was during one of Les Nessman's *WKRP in Cincinnati* crop reports. It turns out, I was really missing out on something. With a taste somewhere between a turnip and a sweet potato, the rutabaga is a severely under-loved tuber. Be different! Smash a rutabaga, today!

—Greg

- 2 qt water
- 3 tsp salt, divided
- 2 large rutabagas, peeled, cut into 1-inch chunks
- 2 eggs, beaten
- ½ cup cream
- ¼ cup bread crumbs
- 2 Tbsp brown sugar
- ½ tsp ground nutmeg
- 3 Tbsp butter, divided

Preheat the oven to 350°F.

Bring water and 2 teaspoons salt to a boil. Add rutabaga pieces, and boil until cooked through, about 20 minutes. Drain and transfer rutabaga pieces to a large mixing bowl.

Using a potato masher, ricer, or the paddle of a standing mixer, mash the rutabagas until smooth.

In a separate mixing bowl, combine eggs, cream, bread crumbs, brown sugar, the remaining 1 teaspoon of salt, and the nutmeg. Stir until combined evenly. Pour this mixture into the larger mixing bowl with the rutabagas and stir until combined evenly.

Grease a baking dish with 1 tablespoon of butter. Pour the rutabaga mix into the dish and place in the preheated oven for 60 minutes, or until the top is browned. Serve while hot, topped with additional melted butter.

Caramelized Cabbage Meatloaf (Kålpudding)

SWEDEN

TOTAL TIME: 1 hour, 15 minutes
CHARACTER: Main
VESSEL: 9 x 13 inch baking dish, or equivalent
SERVES: 4-6

My Eastern European grandmother used to make the best *cholopshkes*. Firm meatballs, each wrapped in buttery cabbage, and braised in an oh-so-1950s ketchup-based sauce. My question is, how did those darn Swedes get hold of Grandma's recipe? Sure, they replaced the ketchup with lingonberry. Yeah, they shredded and caramelized the cabbage. Okay, they made it into one big casserole. But they can't fool me. Sneaky Swedes.

—Greg

4 Tbsp butter, divided
1 onion, diced
½ head (about 1½ pounds) green cabbage, cored, shredded
1½ tsp salt, divided
1½ Tbsp molasses
½ cup water
½ lb ground veal
½ lb ground pork
1 shallot, minced
1 clove garlic, minced
¼ cup bread crumbs
¼ cup heavy cream
¼ cup chicken broth
1 egg
½ tsp ground black pepper
Lingonberry, cranberry, or pomegranate preserves for serving

Preheat the oven to 375°F.

Place a large skillet over medium heat. Add 3 tablespoons of butter. When the butter has melted, add onion and sauté for 6-8 minutes, or until the onion is translucent. Increase heat to high, and add the cabbage and 1 teaspoon of salt to the skillet. Continue to sauté until all the cabbage has wilted, an additional 6-7 minutes.

continued on page 154

Add water and molasses to the skillet. Reduce to the heat to medium-low and simmer for 14-16 minutes, stirring occasionally. When the liquid has mostly evaporated and the cabbage has browned, remove from heat and reserve.

While the cabbage is simmering, in a large mixing bowl, thoroughly combine the remaining ingredients, including the remaining ½ teaspoon of salt. This will make a moist, sticky meatloaf mixture.

Using the 1 remaining tablespoon of butter, coat the insides of a baking dish. Place half of the cabbage mixture in an even layer at the bottom of the baking dish. Then, add the meatloaf mixture, pressing down lightly to make it an even layer, and to flatten the cabbage below. Lastly, top with the remaining half of the cabbage mixture.

Transfer the baking dish to the oven and roast for 45-50 minutes, or until the cabbage on top is browned and getting crispy. Remove the kålpudding from the oven and serve hot scoops with a small dollop of the fruit preserves.

Sheepless Shepherd's Pie

ENGLAND

TOTAL TIME: 1 hour, 45 minutes
CHARACTER: One Pot Meal, Main, Side
VESSEL: 9 x 13 inch baking dish, or equivalent
SERVES: 6-8

Shepherd's pie is beloved as a pub staple across the UK. The silky, savory, succulent filling foiled by the creamy, luscious, fluffy topping. There are very few dishes that simultaneously fulfill the mind, belly, and soul in such a charming way. That is . . . until you visit your darned doctor who tells you to lay off the red meat for a while. *If it has no sheep, can I still call it shepherd's pie, Doctor?* I kid! This dish can stand up to the baaaa-d version, any day of the week.

—Howie

TOPPING:

3-4 (about 2 lb) russet potatoes, peeled, cut into 1-inch chunks

2 qt water

1 Tbsp plus ½ tsp salt, divided

4 Tbsp butter, melted

1 cup heavy cream or milk

2 eggs, beaten

½ tsp ground black pepper

FILLING:

2 Tbsp extra-virgin olive oil

1 medium onion, diced

2 medium carrots, peeled, cut into ½ inch rounds

20 oz mixed mushrooms (cremini, shiitake, button, etc.), stemmed and thinly sliced

1 tsp salt

2 Tbsp all-purpose flour

3 cloves garlic, minced

2 Tbsp tomato paste

1 tsp paprika

1 tsp dried oregano

¾ cup parsley, chopped, divided

½ tsp black pepper

¾ cup frozen peas

1½ cups vegetable broth or stock

1 Tbsp soy sauce

Preheat the oven to 400°F.

To prepare the filling, place a skillet over medium heat. Add olive oil. When the oil begins to shimmer, add the onion and carrots and sauté 4–5 minutes, until the onion begins to brown. Add

continued on page 157

mushrooms, continuing to sauté for another 8-10 minutes, until mushrooms are tender and have released most of their moisture.

Sprinkle the flour on top of this mixture, stir it in and sauté for 1 minute. Add garlic, tomato paste, paprika, oregano, ½ cup of the parsley, and pepper, and sauté until fragrant, about 30 seconds. Add peas, broth, and soy sauce, and bring to a boil. Reduce heat to low and simmer for 20 minutes, until the broth has thickened to the consistency of gravy. Remove the skillet from the heat, and transfer this mixture into a baking dish, and let it cool while you prepare the topping.

To prepare the topping, in a medium or large pot, add the potatoes and water to cover. Add 1 tablespoon of the salt to the water. Bring to a boil over high heat and then turn heat down to keep pot at a simmer. Cook until you can easily pierce a potato chunk with a knife, about 8-10 minutes.

Drain potatoes and transfer them to a large bowl. Use either a potato masher or ricer to crush potatoes into an even consistency. Stir butter and cream or milk into potatoes. When the potatoes have cooled a bit, about 10 minutes, whisk in the eggs and remaining ½ teaspoon of salt.

Using a spatula, evenly spread the mashed potato topping on top of mixture in the baking dish. Be sure that the topping is spread to edges of the baking dish and covers the filling completely. Place the baking dish in the middle rack of the oven. In the rack beneath the baking dish, place an empty baking sheet to catch any filling that might sneak by and overflow during baking. Bake for 25-30 minutes or until the mashed potatoes begin to brown.

Remove the casserole from the oven and allow to cool for 15 minutes. Sprinkle the top with the remaining ¼ cup of parsley before serving in bowls.

Cured Salmon Potato Casserole (Laxpudding)

SWEDEN

TOTAL TIME: 1 hour, 30 minutes
CHARACTER: Side
VESSEL: 9 x 13 inch baking dish, or equivalent
SERVES: 6-8

This dish came to me on a trip to Switzerland. Yes, the dish is Swedish, but they both start with the same two letters. Anyhow, Laxpudding is a unique casserole that not only sends the basic cured salmon into another universe when it meets potatoes and cream . . . The dish changes the character of all the players. Cook it and you will understand. Simple complexity that words cannot describe.

—Howie

1 Tbsp extra-virgin olive oil
5-6 (about 2½-3 lb) russet potatoes, peeled, sliced ⅛-inch thick (a mandoline helps)
1 lb gravlax or smoked salmon, divided
4 Tbsp dill, chopped, divided
3 cups half-and-half or cream
5 large eggs
1 tsp salt
1 tsp ground black pepper
1 cup sour cream

Preheat the oven to 375°F. Coat the bottom and sides of a baking dish with olive oil.

Form a layer using a third of the potato slices along the bottom of the baking dish, overlapping them like shingles. Then, use half the salmon to form a layer on top of the potatoes. Sprinkle 1 tablespoon of dill on top. Repeat with another layer of a third of the potato slices, the remaining salmon, and another 1 tablespoon of dill. Top with remaining potato.

In a large mixing bowl, whisk together cream, eggs, salt, and pepper. Slowly pour over the potatoes, giving it some time to fall to the bottom of the baking dish. Sprinkle 1 tablespoon dill across the top. Cover the baking dish tightly with aluminum foil and transfer to the oven for 40 minutes. Remove from the oven, discard the foil, and return to the oven, uncovered, for 20-25 minutes or until the top begins to brown.

In a small mixing bowl, stir together sour cream and the remaining dill.

Remove the casserole from the oven and allow it to cool for 10-15 minutes. Serve with a dollop of dill sour cream.

Chicken and Leek Pie

ENGLAND

TOTAL TIME: 1 hour, 30 minutes
CHARACTER: One Pot Meal, Main
VESSEL: 8 x 8 inch baking dish, 4 ramekins, or equivalent
SERVES: 4-6

> Little Jack Mitchin
> Sat in his kitchen
> Eating a chicken pie.
> He snuck in a peek
> And spied a chopped leek
> And said "This is good, that's no lie."
>
> —Greg

1 sheet frozen puff pastry
4 Tbsp (½ stick) butter
2 leeks, halved lengthwise, cut into 2-inch segments
½ tsp ground black pepper
½ tsp paprika
3 tsp chicken bouillon powder or paste
¼ cup flour
2 cups heavy cream
⅓ cup + 1 Tbsp water, divided
1½ lb chicken breasts, boneless, skinless, diced
1 large egg

Remove puff pastry sheet from the freezer and allow to thaw, folded on the counter, for about 30 minutes.

Preheat the oven to 375°F.

Place a skillet over medium heat. Add butter. When the butter has melted, add the leeks, pepper, paprika, and bouillon powder, and sauté for 6-8 minutes, or until the leeks have softened. Sprinkle the flour over the leeks and continue to sauté until the flour is no longer visible, about 2-3 minutes.

Whisk in the cream and ⅓ cup of water, making sure it is fully incorporated with no flour or bullion lumps. Bring the mixture to a boil and reduce the heat to low. Stir the chicken pieces into the cream sauce and allow it to simmer for 6 minutes, stirring occasionally. Turn off the heat.

Dust the counter or board with flour, unfold the puff pastry and place the sheet atop the flour, and dust with some more flour. Roll the sheet into a 10-inch square, smoothing out all the fold seams.

Transfer the contents of the skillet to a single baking dish or ramekins. Cover the vessel(s) with thawed pastry, pinching to seal the edges of the baking dish. Cut a couple of small slits in the pie crust to allow steam to escape. Beat the egg and the remaining 1 tablespoon of water together. Using a pastry brush, paint the top of the pastry with egg wash.

Transfer the baking dish(es) to the oven and bake for 35-40 minutes, or until the crust has browned and risen. Remove the pie(s) from the oven and allow them to rest for 10 minutes before serving.

Short Rib Stew-sserole
(Stew na hÉireann)
IRELAND

TOTAL TIME: 2 hours, 15 minutes
CHARACTER: One Pot Meal, Main
VESSEL: 9 x 13 inch baking dish, or equivalent
SERVES: 6-8

4 Tbsp butter
2 lb beef short ribs, cut into 2-inch pieces
2½ tsp salt, divided
1 large onion, diced
5 stalks celery, thinly sliced
12 oz baby carrots, halved
5 Tbsp flour
3 cloves garlic
4 cups beef stock or broth
3 Tbsp soy sauce
2-3 (about 1½ lb) russet potatoes, cut into ¼ inch slices
3 scallions, thinly sliced

> The word "stew" could use a marketing campaign. Stew is delicious. It's healthy. There's no reason not to love it. Yet, when was the last time you went into a restaurant and said "Oooh, I really want the stew." I'll tell you when—never. And that needs to change. The journey of a thousand miles begins with one step. And one new "stew." Take that step with me. Step forward with me into a new world dominated by *stew-sserole!*
>
> —Greg

Preheat the oven to 325°F.

Place a skillet over medium heat. Add butter. Once melted, add the beef and 1 teaspoon of salt, and sauté 6-8 minutes, until the all of the beef has browned. Using a slotted spoon, remove the beef to a baking dish, leaving any juices behind. Add onion, celery, carrots, and 1 teaspoon of salt to the skillet, and sauté for 6-8 minutes or until the onion pieces are translucent.

Sprinkle the flour on top of this mixture, stir it in, and sauté for 2 minutes. Add garlic and sauté until fragrant, about 30 seconds. Add stock or broth and soy sauce and bring to a boil. Reduce heat to low and simmer for 5 minutes, until the broth has thickened to the consistency of gravy. Transfer the skillet contents to the baking dish atop the beef.

Arrange the potato slices atop the mixture in the baking dish in a tile pattern, slightly overlapping one another to cover the surface. Tightly cover the baking dish with aluminum foil and transfer to the oven and roast for one hour. Carefully remove the foil and continue to roast for an additional 30 minutes. Remove the casserole from the oven, garnish with scallions, and serve hot scoops into bowls—be sure to include all the good bits!

Steak and Stout Pie

(Stéig agus Stout Pie)

IRELAND

TOTAL TIME: 2 hours, 30 minutes
CHARACTER: One Pot Meal, Main
VESSEL: 8 x 8 inch baking dish, 4 small ramekins, or equivalent
SERVES: 4-6

1 sheet frozen pie dough
2 Tbsp all-purpose flour
½ tsp salt
¼ tsp black pepper
1½ lb beef chuck, cut into 1-inch pieces
2 Tbsp vegetable oil
1 onion, diced
2 cups mushrooms, sliced
3 cloves garlic, minced
2 Tbsp tomato paste
1 cup Irish stout or other dark beer
1 cup + 1 Tbsp water, divided
1 Tbsp Worcestershire sauce
¼ tsp dried thyme
1 large egg

I often wonder about the origin of this delicious pie. I mean, how many pints of stout do you need to consume before you 1) spill your drink into your buddy's pot pie, and 2) convince yourself that he won't notice on his next bite? Or, more precisely, how many pints does it take to reach the Goldilocks zone, where you're tipsy enough to spill the beer, but lucid enough to remember it the next morning, when you decide to write up this recipe? Well, there's only one way to tell. Somebody, pass me a Guinness.

—Greg

Thaw the frozen pie dough, as directed by the package.

In a small mixing bowl, combine the flour, salt, and pepper. Dip beef pieces into the seasoned flour, turning to coat. Shake off excess and reserve beef on a plate.

Place a skillet over medium-high heat. Add vegetable oil. When the oil begins to shimmer, add half of the meat, and sauté until browned, about 7-8 minutes. Using a slotted spoon, remove the beef to a plate and repeat with the rest of the meat.

Into the empty skillet, add the onion and sauté until almost translucent, about 4-6 minutes. Add the mushrooms and continue to sauté for another 4-6 minutes. Add the garlic and tomato paste

continued on page 166

and sauté until fragrant, about 1 minute. Add the beer and 1 cup of water, then use a spatula to free any browned bits from the bottom of the skillet. Add Worcestershire sauce, thyme, and the reserved beef, and stir to combine. Bring the liquid to a boil, reduce the heat to low, and simmer for 60-70 minutes.

Turn off the heat and allow the stew to cool for at least 30 minutes. Preheat oven to 350°F.

Transfer the contents of the skillet to a single baking dish, or to 4-6 ramekins. Cover the baking dish(es) with thawed pie crust, pinching to seal the edges of the baking dish, and cutting a few slits along the top. Beat the egg and 1 tablespoon of water together. Using a pastry brush, paint the top of the dough with egg wash.

Transfer the baking dish(es) to the oven and bake for 45-50 minutes, or until the crust has browned. Remove the pot pies from the oven and allow them to rest for 10 minutes before serving.

Pumpernickel Pudding
(Pumpernickel Strata)
GERMANY

TOTAL TIME: 2 hours, 30 minutes
CHARACTER: Side
VESSEL: 9 x 13 inch baking dish, or equivalent
SERVES: 6-8

4 Tbsp butter, divided
1 medium white onion, diced
2 tsp salt, divided
5 cups (about 1 lb) Swiss chard, ribs removed, chopped
6 cups (about 1½ lb) pumpernickel bread, toasted, cubed
1 red bell pepper, roasted, peeled, diced
½ cup kalamata or other black olives, pitted
7 eggs
2 cups half-and-half or milk
1 Tbsp dried thyme
1 tsp garlic powder
1 Tbsp Dijon mustard
4 cups Gouda cheese, shredded, divided

> Having grown up in New York and New Jersey around Jewish, German, and German-Jewish delis, I know a thing or two about pumpernickel. Deep, dark brown bread, perhaps most familiar as a bagel, comes in many forms and I love them all. As I ventured West, the pumpernickel got lighter and lighter until I reached California and it was basically rye bread. This recipe is a German ode to the delis of my youth, to nearly pitch-black bread, and to Californians, for whom I am forever sorry that someone turned your pumpernickel from an 11 down to a 3.
>
> —Howie

Preheat the oven to 325°F.

Place a skillet over medium heat and add 1 tablespoon of butter. When the butter has melted, add onion and 1 teaspoon salt, and sauté until translucent, about 6-8 minutes. Add the Swiss chard and continue to sauté until the greens have completely wilted, about another 6-8 minutes. Turn off the heat.

In a large mixing bowl, toss the bread cubes with the roasted red pepper, olives, and the contents of the skillet. In another mixing bowl, whisk together eggs, half-and-half or milk, thyme, garlic powder, mustard, and remaining 1 teaspoon of salt.

continued on page 169

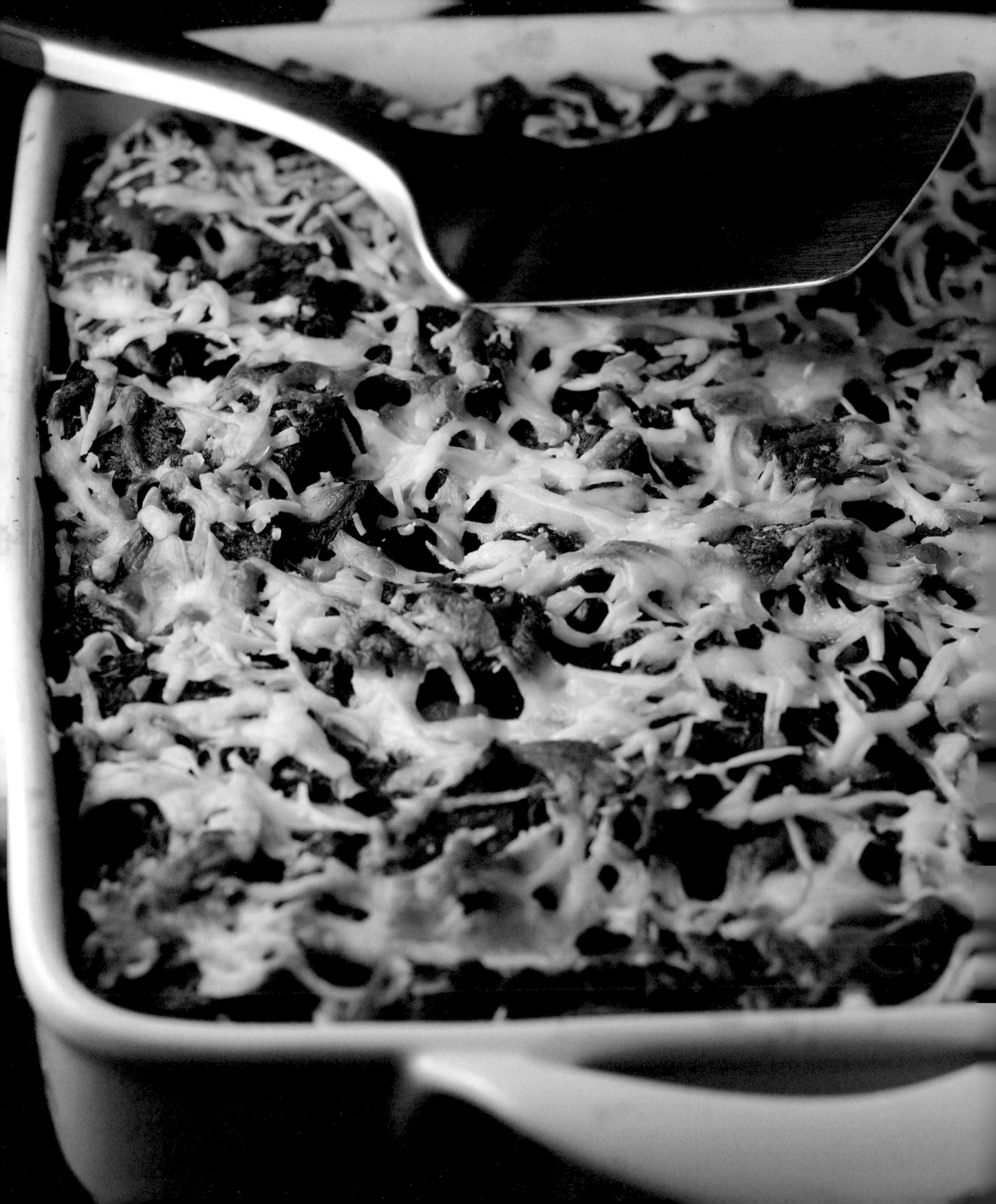

Grease the bottom and sides of a baking dish with 1 tablespoon of butter. Pour half of the bread mixture into the baking dish. Be sure you have one even layer with a flat top (no bread hills). Sprinkle 2 cups of cheese on top of the bread. Top with the remainder of the bread mixture.

Slowly pour the egg mixture evenly over the bread mixture, being sure that some of the liquid reaches most, if not all, of the bread. Use the back of a wooden spoon, a clean hand, or spatula, to compress the whole mixture and ensure that the liquid is evenly distributed.

Cover with plastic wrap and allow the baking dish to sit on the counter for an hour, undisturbed. It needs its beauty sleep. Remove the plastic wrap, sprinkle the top with the remaining 2 cups of cheese and dot with the remaining 2 tablespoons of butter. Transfer the baking dish to the center rack of the oven and bake for 50-55 minutes, or until the top is beginning to brown and get crusty.

Remove the casserole from the oven and serve in slices or scoops, hot.

Ham and Potato Cake
(Rösti)
SWITZERLAND

TOTAL TIME: 1 hour, 45 minutes
CHARACTER: Side
VESSEL: 9 x 13 inch baking dish, or equivalent
SERVES: 6-8

3-4 (about 2½ lb) russet, Yukon Gold, or other baking potatoes, peeled
3 qt water, + more for an ice bath
1 small onion, grated and drained
4 Tbsp extra-virgin olive oil, divided
8 oz ham steak, diced
½ cup sour cream
2 Tbsp Dijon mustard
2 tsp salt
1 tsp ground black pepper

> You may notice that Greg also has a recipe for "Rösti" in this book. It would be better if you didn't notice this. In fact, you should rip that page out of the book, set it on fire, and scatter the ashes to the four winds. Why, you may ask? He puts cheese in his rösti. Let me say that again. He. Puts. Cheese. In. His. Rösti. I believe this leads to arrest in some parts of the Alps. Ask Greg if he's even stepped foot in Switzerland. Go ahead, ask him.
>
> —Howie

Preheat the oven to 400°F. Position an oven rack in the lower third of the oven.

In a large pot, add potatoes and water, and bring to a rolling boil over high heat. Reduce heat to medium-low and simmer 5 more minutes. Using a slotted spoon, remove the potatoes and place them in an ice water bath for 15-20 minutes, or until you can handle them for shredding.

In a large mixing bowl, whisk together remaining ingredients, except for 2 tablespoons of the olive oil. Remove the potatoes from the ice bath and pat dry. Shred using a box grater. Fold into the mixing bowl with the other ingredients.

Coat the bottom and sides of a baking dish with 2 tablespoons oil. Scatter the potato mixture into the baking dish. Gently flatten the top, being sure not to make the layer very dense. Drizzle the top with the remaining 1 tablespoon of olive oil.

Transfer the baking dish to the lower third of the oven and roast for 1 hour and 15 minutes, or until the top is nicely browned and crispy. Serve hot scoops and include some of the crispy top and bottom with every serving.

Ham and Cheese Potato Cake
(Rösti v2)

SWITZERLAND (in Greg's dreams)

TOTAL TIME: 1 hour, 45 minutes
CHARACTER: Side
VESSEL: 8 x 8 inch baking dish, or equivalent
SERVES: 4-6

> Ok, I'll admit it. Howie has been to Switzerland. I've never even owned a Swatch. So, his version is certainly more authentic. But mine is clearly better. I mean—ham, eggs, and cheese on top of crisp hash browns. This is the Promised Land on a plate. Nirvana in a pan. Why is he even bothering to compete?
>
> —Greg

2-3 (about 1½ lb) russet potatoes, peeled, shredded
2 Tbsp butter, divided
1 small onion, diced
6 oz ham, diced
½ cup yogurt
6 oz Gruyère or other Swiss cheese, grated
½ tsp salt
½ tsp black pepper
¼ tsp cayenne pepper
5 eggs

Preheat the oven to 400°F. Place potato shreds in a mixing bowl and cover with cold water.

Place a skillet over medium-high heat and add 1 tablespoon butter. Once melted and starting to bubble, add the onion and sauté until translucent, about 6-8 minutes. Add the ham and continue to sauté for 3-4 minutes. Transfer skillet contents to a large mixing bowl.

Drain the potatoes well, squeezing handfuls in a sieve or towel to get the water out. Add them to the mixing bowl with the onion and ham. Add the yogurt, cheese, salt, and peppers to the bowl, and stir to combine.

Place the remaining 1 tablespoon of butter into a baking dish, and place in the oven for 3-5 minutes, or until the butter is melted and bubbling. Carefully remove the baking dish from the oven and spread the potato mixture evenly across the bottom. Return the baking dish to the oven for 30 minutes.

Set the oven to low broil and cook for an additional 4-5 minutes, or until the top begins to brown. Keep a close eye on the potato cake during this to prevent burning. Remove the casserole from the oven and set the temperature back to 400°F.

Using the back of a spoon, make a well in the potato cake. Crack an egg neatly into the well. Repeat with the remaining eggs. Return to the oven and bake for another 10-12 minutes, until whites are set and the yolks are still runny. Serve immediately.

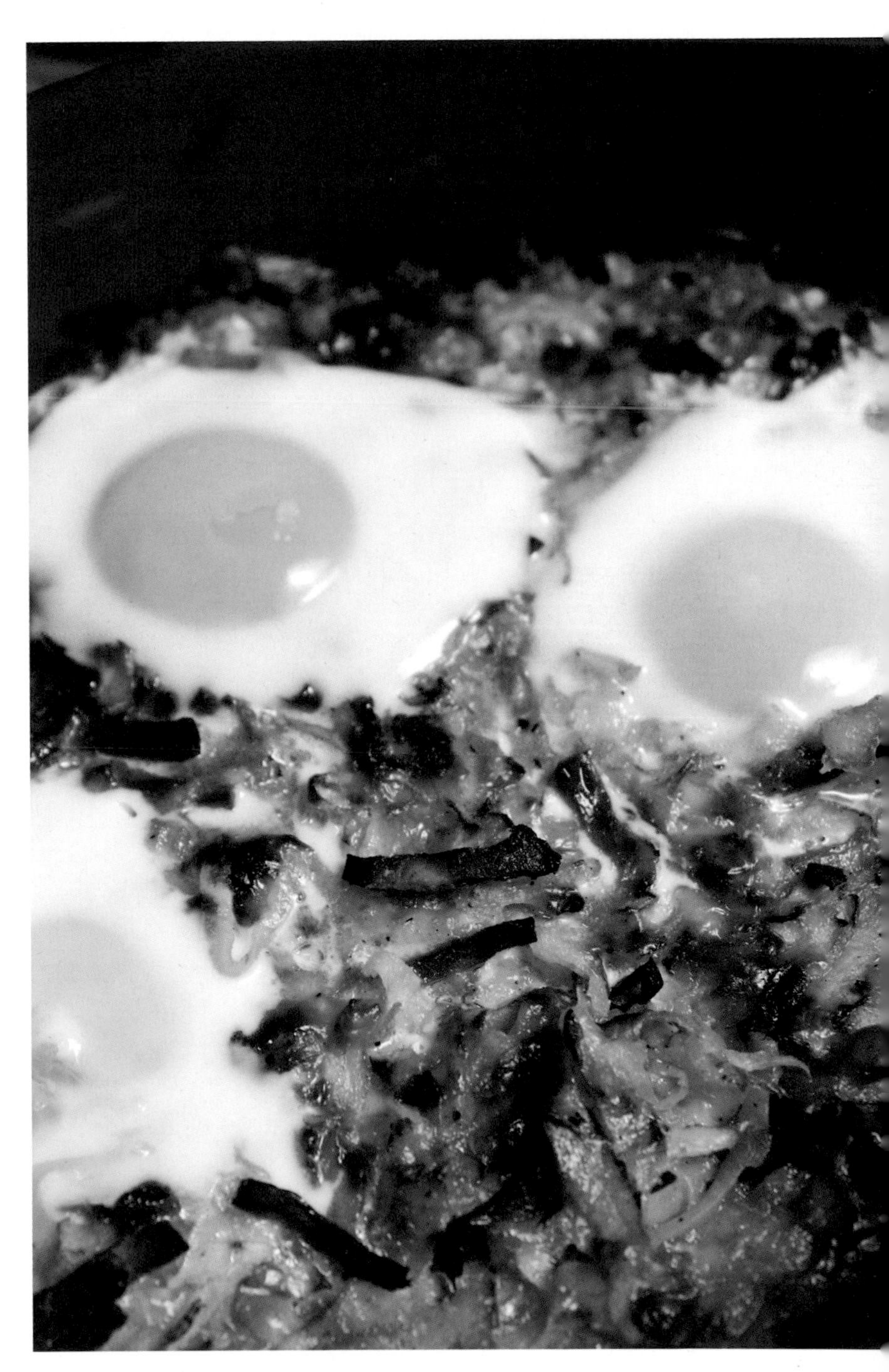

Spinach and Feta Pie
(Spanakopita)
GREECE

TOTAL TIME: 1 hour, 15 minutes
CHARACTER: Side
VESSEL: 9 x 9 inch baking dish, or equivalent
SERVES: 6-8

ASSEMBLY:
20 sheets (about ½ lb) frozen phyllo dough
½ cup extra-virgin olive oil

FILLING:
2 lb spinach, chopped
1 tsp extra-virgin olive oil
6 scallions, thinly sliced
2 cups feta cheese (10 ounces)
½ cup Parmesan cheese, shredded or grated
¼ cup fresh dill, finely chopped
¼ cup parsley, finely chopped
½ tsp salt
¼ tsp nutmeg
2 eggs, beaten

Making spanakopita is a family affair. You need one person manning the phyllo, making sure to keep it covered with a moist towel. Another on oil patrol. A third set of hands on filling duty. And, of course, at least two folders. My family would spend hours hunched over the kitchen table, getting ready for the big Matza picnic. In retrospect, that wasn't too bright. We could have, instead, whipped up a few of these casseroles, and spent the rest of the evening at a Dodger game. Silly us.

—Greg

Preheat the oven to 375°F. Thaw the phyllo, per the package's instructions.

To make the filling, place a large skillet over medium-high heat. Add enough chopped spinach to fill the pan. As the spinach wilts, add more, until all the spinach is cooked and bright green, about 6-8 minutes. Remove cooked spinach to a colander. Once it cools, press down to remove as much liquid as possible.

While the spinach is cooling, add 1 teaspoon of oil to the skillet. When the oil begins to shimmer, add the scallions. Sauté until the scallions are soft, about 3 minutes. In a large bowl, combine the scallions, drained spinach, feta cheese, Parmesan cheese, dill, parsley, salt, and nutmeg. Stir to combine and break up the largest chunks of feta. Add the eggs and continue stirring until combined.

To assemble, begin by brushing a baking dish with 1 teaspoon of olive oil. Place a sheet of phyllo dough along the bottom of the dish. Quickly brush a thin layer of oil, and then stack another sheet of phyllo. Repeat until you've used 10 sheets. Don't worry if the phyllo tears a bit—that's completely normal.

Spread the filling over the bottom 10 sheets of phyllo, then repeat the phyllo process for the top 10 sheets, alternating phyllo and oil. Coat the top sheet of phyllo generously with the last of the olive oil.

Transfer the baking dish to the oven and bake for 25-30 minutes, or until top is browned. Remove the spanakopita from the oven and allow it to cool for 10 minutes, then slice and serve in triangles.

Layered Eggplant Casserole (Moussaka)

GREECE

TOTAL TIME: 2 hours
CHARACTER: Main
VESSEL: 9 x 13 inch baking dish, or equivalent
SERVES: 8-10

> A great moussaka is a symphony on the palate. Melodically melty on the inside, a crusty crescendo on the outside. The brooding baritone of the eggplant playing off of a light tenor of the tomatoes. And topped with the blaring horns and steady backbeat of béchamel sauce! I guess I lost the metaphor there. But, then again, I always preferred ska to classical, so let's try this again. A great moussaka is the Mighty Mighty Bosstones of Greek food.
>
> —Greg

EGGPLANT:

3 medium (about 2 lb) eggplants, peeled, cut into ¾ inch slices
3 Tbsp extra-virgin olive oil
½ tsp salt

MEAT SAUCE:

1 Tbsp extra-virgin olive oil
1 large onion, chopped
1½ tsp salt
2 cloves garlic, minced
2 lb ground beef
1 15-oz can pureed tomatoes
2 Tbsp tomato paste
½ cup red wine
2 Tbsp parsley, chopped
1 tsp sugar
½ tsp cinnamon
½ tsp ground black pepper
½ cup water

WHITE SAUCE:

2½ cups milk
8 Tbsp butter
½ cup flour
¼ tsp cinnamon
½ tsp salt
¼ tsp black pepper
3 eggs, separated
1½ cups grated Parmesan cheese, divided

continued on page 178

Preheat oven to 450°F.

In a large mixing bowl, combine the eggplant, olive oil, and salt. Toss the eggplant to coat. Place the eggplant on a sheet pan in a single layer. Transfer the sheet pan to the oven and roast for 15-20 minutes, or until the eggplant is soft and beginning to brown. Remove the eggplant from the oven and set the oven 350°F.

While the eggplant is roasting, begin the meat sauce. Place a skillet over medium-high heat, and add the olive oil. Once the oil begins to shimmer, add onion and salt to the skillet and sauté for 6-8 minutes, or until the onion begins to become translucent. Add garlic and continue to sauté until fragrant, about 30 seconds. Add the ground beef and continue to sauté, using a spatula to break up the largest chunks. Cook for 8-10 minutes, or until the meat is browned.

Add the tomatoes, tomato paste, wine, parsley, sugar, cinnamon, ground pepper, and water. Bring to a boil, then lower the heat to a light simmer. Allow the sauce to simmer, uncovered, for 30 minutes.

Next, assemble the casserole, by spreading a third of your eggplant across the bottom of a baking dish. Spread half the meat sauce over the eggplant. Repeat with a second layer of eggplant and meat sauce, topped with the last third of the eggplant.

To prepare your white sauce, start by warming your milk to about 150 degrees—about 1½ minutes in the microwave or a similar time in a pan. While the milk is warming, heat a skillet over medium heat and add butter. When it has completely melted, sprinkle in the flour and whisk to combine completely. Continue to whisk the mixture for 3-4 minutes, until you have a blond roux.

Slowly pour in 2 cups of the milk while continuing to whisk briskly, to ensure the sauce is smooth with no lumps. Stir in 1 cup of the cheese, along with the salt, pepper and cinnamon. Reduce the heat to low and let the mixture simmer, stirring occasionally for 3-5 minutes.

While the mixture is simmering beat the egg whites until fluffy, about 20 seconds with a mixer or 2 minutes with a whisk. Stop before they begin to form soft peaks. (we're looking for some airiness, but not a meringue). Stir the remaining ½ cup of warm milk into your egg yolks, to temper them. Add the yolks to the skillet and stir to combine. Remove the skillet from the heat, and fold in the egg whites until well combined.

Pour the white sauce over the top of the meat sauce, completely covering the casserole. Sprinkle the top with the remaining ½ cup of Parmesan cheese.

Transfer the baking dish to the oven and bake for 50-60 minutes, or until the top is lightly browned. Remove from the oven and allow to cool for at least 15 minutes prior to cutting and serving.

"Don't Call It Pastitsio" Baked Macaroni

(Makarónia tou Foúrnou)

CYPRUS

TOTAL TIME: 2 hours, 15 minutes
CHARACTER: One Pot Meal, Main, Side
VESSEL: 11 x 15 inch baking dish, or equivalent
SERVES: 8-10

I have a good Cypriot friend whom I consulted while refining our pastitsio recipe. Every conversation began like this: I'm going to make pastitsio, let's chat. *Don't call it pastitsio. It's makarónia tou foúrnou, baked pasta!* Well, isn't this one special? Don't you have many other baked pasta dishes in Cyprus? *Yes, it is special, so we call this one makarónia tou foúrnou, and have other names for the other ones.* But why not call pastitsio pastitsio? *Because we call it makarónia tou foúrnou.* Dear reader, you and I now have the same level of understanding. Enjoy this pastitsio.

—Howie

MEAT SAUCE:

2 Tbsp extra-virgin olive oil, divided
1 large onion, diced
2 lb ground beef, pork, or lamb
2 tsp salt
1 tsp ground black pepper
1 28-oz can pureed tomatoes
1 Tbsp dried oregano
10 leaves mint, chopped
2 cloves garlic, minced
1 tsp ground cinnamon
¾ cup parsley, chopped, divided

PASTA:

4 qt water
1 lb penne (or other tube) pasta
2 Tbsp salt

WHITE SAUCE:

4 Tbsp (½ stick) butter
¼ cup flour
2 cups milk
1 tsp salt
1 tsp ground black pepper
¾ cup sour cream
1 cup Parmesan cheese, grated or shredded
2 eggs

continued on page 181

Preheat the oven to 375°F.

To make the meat sauce, heat a skillet over medium high heat. Add 1 tablespoon of olive oil. When the oil begins to shimmer, add the onion and cook until lightly browned around the edges, about 4–6 minutes. Add the meat, salt, and pepper. Continue to sauté, breaking up the meat with a spatula. Cook until the meat is no longer pink, about 6–8 minutes.

Carefully pour in the tomatoes, add oregano, mint, garlic, cinnamon, ½ cup of parsley, and stir in evenly. Reduce the heat to medium-low and simmer the meat sauce while you cook the pasta and the white sauce.

In a large pot, bring water to a rolling boil over high heat. Add pasta and salt. Cook for 10 minutes, stirring occasionally to ensure the pasta does not stick to the pot. Drain the pasta, and rinse with cold water to ensure the pasta does not overcook. Set aside.

As the pasta water comes to a boil and as the pasta cooks, make the white sauce. Heat a skillet over medium heat and add butter. When it melts completely, sprinkle in the flour and whisk to combine completely. Continue to whisk the mixture for 2 minutes.

Slowly pour in the milk while continuing to whisk briskly, to ensure the sauce is smooth with no lumps. Stir in salt and pepper. Reduce the heat to low and let the mixture simmer, stirring occasionally for 8 minutes. Remove the mixture to a large mixing bowl, stir in sour cream, then the Parmesan cheese and eggs. Mix thoroughly.

Coat the bottom and sides of a baking dish with the remaining 1 tablespoon of olive oil. Give the pasta a good shake to get as much of the water off as possible. Pour the drained pasta evenly into the bottom of the baking dish. Next, pour the meat sauce evenly on top of the pasta. Finally, slowly pour the white sauce over the meat sauce evenly, making sure not to disturb the meat sauce too much, as you want a finished casserole in fairly distinct layers.

Transfer the baking dish to the oven, and bake for 40-45 minutes or until the top is golden brown. Allow the casserole to rest for 15-20 minutes before serving in blocks.

Lemony Rice and Grape Leaf Casserole

(Pilaf Dolmatia)

GREECE

TOTAL TIME: 1 hour
CHARACTER: Side
VESSEL: 9 x 13 inch baking dish, or equivalent
SERVES: 4-6

1 cup Greek-style yogurt
1 tsp salt
3 Tbsp fresh dill, roughly chopped
3 Tbsp fresh mint, roughly chopped
¼ cup fresh parsley, roughly chopped
½ cup marinated artichoke hearts, roughly chopped
1 tsp lemon zest
Juice of 1 lemon
2 cups cooked white rice
20 jarred grape leaves
1 Tbsp extra-virgin olive oil

> When I was fifteen, I spent a few days on a kibbutz in Israel. Some might have called the days spent clearing rocks volunteer work. Some might have called it forced child labor. My reward? One day working in the vineyard, pruning and training the vines. As the child of a Greek family, I was in heaven. The smell of the grape leaves was intoxicating. I even ate some of them raw, which won me quite a few stares. Stare away—you don't know what you are missing.
>
> —Greg

Preheat the oven to 350°F.

In a mixing bowl, combine the yogurt, salt, dill, mint, parsley, artichokes, lemon zest, and lemon juice. Stir until well combined. Fold in the rice until fully incorporated.

Prepare the grape leaves by rinsing them well and using scissors to trim the thick stem at the base of each leaf. Take 5 large leaves and chop them into ¼-inch strips. Mix the leaf strips into the rice mixture.

Line the bottom of a baking dish with 6-8 grape leaves—they will overlap. Using a pastry brush, gently paint the leaves with olive oil. Using a rubber spatula, evenly spread the rice and yogurt mixture over the layer of leaves. Top with a final layer of grape leaves, painting the top generously with the remaining olive oil.

Transfer the baking dish to the oven and roast for 25-30 minutes, or until the top leaves crisp up.

Remove the casserole from the oven and allow it to rest for at least 15 minutes before using a knife to slice into cubes. Serve warm or at room temperature.

Toasted Noodle Ham and Spinach Bake

(Fideos en la Cazuela con Jamón)

SPAIN

TOTAL TIME: 45 minutes
CHARACTER: One Pot Meal, Main, Side
VESSEL: 9 x 13 inch baking dish, or equivalent
SERVES: 6-8

> Don't worry. The spinach in this one makes it a totally healthy dish. Trust me. Really, really, really healthy. I mean, would Popeye lie to you?
>
> —Greg

4 Tbsp extra-virgin olive oil, divided
12 oz #2 fideo, or other very thin dried pasta, broken into 1-inch pieces
2 (about ½ cup) shallots, minced
1 lb ham, sliced thinly
4 cloves garlic, minced
12 oz baby spinach, roughly chopped
2 Tbsp tomato paste
3 cups chicken broth

Preheat the oven to 400°F.

In a baking dish, combine the noodles with 3 tablespoons of the olive oil. Toss to combine. Place in the oven, for 12-14 minutes, tossing halfway through. Noodles are done when they are toasted to a light brown.

While the noodles are toasting, place a skillet over medium-high heat and add the remaining 1 tablespoon of olive oil. When the oil begins to shimmer, add shallots and sauté for 3-5 minutes, or until lightly browned. Add ham and continue to sauté for another 5 minutes, until the edges of the ham begin to brown.

Next, add garlic and sauté until fragrant, about 30 seconds. Add spinach and tomato paste, continuing to sauté until the spinach is wilted, about 1 minute. Turn off the heat and add the chicken broth, stirring to combine the tomato paste into the broth.

When the noodles are toasted, remove the baking dish from the oven. Carefully pour the ham and spinach broth over the noodles and tightly cover the baking dish with aluminum foil. Return the baking dish to the oven and bake for 10 minutes.

Remove the baking dish from the oven and remove the foil. Stir the noodles with the ham and spinach, and return to the oven, uncovered. Cook another 2-3 minutes, or until the broth is fully absorbed and the noodles are mostly cooked through. Allow it to rest for 5 minutes, during which the noodles will complete cooking.

Shellfish Rice Casserole
(Paella Mariscos)
SPAIN

TOTAL TIME: 50 minutes
CHARACTER: One Pot Meal
VESSEL: 12 inch cast iron skillet, or other oven-safe skillet
SERVES: 6-8

> I took Spanish throughout high school. My classroom name was Pepe. I was a terrific student. Since then, I've forgotten nearly everything about Spanish except for the food words. Go figure. Anyhow, here is your pronunciation lesson for today. *Pah-Eh-Ya*. Makes you smile, doesn't it?
>
> —Howie

2½ cups water
2 Tbsp soy sauce
½ lb shrimp, peeled, deveined, shells and heads kept
¼ cup extra-virgin olive oil
3 scallions, thinly sliced
2 4-oz cans roasted green chiles (hot or mild)
2 cloves garlic, minced
1 tsp salt
1 tsp ground black pepper
2 tsp smoked paprika
1½ cup bomba, Arborio, or other short grain rice, uncooked
1 large tomato, halved, grated into a bowl, skin discarded
½ cup dry sherry
1 pinch saffron, crumbled
3 sea scallops, halved, or 12 oz bay scallops
10 mussels in their shell, cleaned, de-bearded
1 cup peas, frozen, thawed
1 red pepper, roasted, peeled, thin strips
1 lemon, cut into wedges

Preheat the oven to 375°F. Arrange a rack in the lower third of the oven.

In a small pot on the stove, bring the water and soy sauce to a boil, lower to a simmer and add the shells and heads from the peeled shrimp. Set the raw shrimp meat aside. Cook the stock for 20 minutes while you prep the rest of the ingredients.

Place a cast iron skillet over medium heat, and add the olive oil. When the oil begins to shimmer, add scallions and chiles and sauté for 3 minutes. Add garlic, salt, pepper, paprika, and rice, and sauté for 2-3 more minutes, or until the rice develops a nutty aroma.

Add tomato, sherry, and saffron to the skillet, and allow the liquid to reduce until it's almost gone, about 4-5 minutes. Strain the shrimp stock of its shells, and carefully pour the liquid into the skillet. Bring the mixture to a boil, lower the heat to low, and simmer for 10-12 minutes, or until the rice is no longer soupy, but still wet.

Top the rice mixture with shrimp, scallops, and mussels, and transfer the skillet to the lower third of the oven. Roast for 10-15 minutes, or until the liquid had been absorbed and the rice is fully cooked, the shrimp is pink, and the mussels have opened up. Remove the skillet from the oven. If the conditions above aren't met, cover the skillet with a lid or foil and allow it to rest for 10 minutes.

Top with peas, roasted pepper, and serve piping hot directly into bowls. Offer a squeeze of lemon with every serving.

Eggplant Parmesan
(Parmigiana di Melanzane)

ITALY

TOTAL TIME: 1 hour, 20 minutes
CHARACTER: Main, Side
VESSEL: 9 x 13 inch baking dish, or equivalent
SERVES: 6-8

I grew up around a lot of Italians, most of Neapolitan descent. A constant source of noise, entertainment, angst, and of course, debate, was how to properly prepare the eggplant for Parmigiana. This cousin peels the eggplant. That cousin only uses egg. This cousin doesn't fry the eggplant, crazy guy bakes it. That cousin salts it, this cousin soaks it! It's fun yet exhausting to hear, but the results always taste like family to me. Here is a method that needs no debate, as it comes from Sicily. Those Sicilians. They have a way of ending an argument.

—Howie

3 medium eggplants, cut into ¼-inch wide slices
2 Tbsp + 1 tsp salt
⅓ cup extra-virgin olive oil, divided
1 large white onion, diced
3 Tbsp tomato paste
3 cloves garlic, minced
½ cup red wine
1 28-oz can crushed or pureed tomatoes
½ tsp sugar
1 Tbsp dried oregano
½ cup basil, thin strips, divided
1 cup Parmesan cheese, grated or shredded, divided
1 cup flour
1 lb mozzarella cheese, shredded

Preheat the oven to 350°F. Line a baking sheet with paper towels and lay the eggplant slices flat. Salt both sides of the slices using 2 tablespoons of the salt. If you run out of room on the sheet pan, place another layer of paper towels atop the eggplant and create another layer of salted slices.

While the eggplant is losing some of its water, prepare the tomato sauce. Place a skillet over medium heat and add 2 tablespoons of the olive oil. When the oil begins to shimmer, add onion and remaining 1 teaspoon of salt to the skillet and sauté for 6-8 minutes or until the onion begins to become translucent. Add tomato paste and garlic, and continue to sauté for an additional minute.

continued on page 190

Remove the zucchini from the oven and lower the temperature to 300°F. In a blender or food processor, combine the roasted zucchini, cream, cornstarch, Parmesan cheese, oregano, black pepper, and eggs. Purée until smooth.

Brush the insides of ramekins with melted butter. Evenly distribute the contents of the blender into the ramekins. Place the ramekins into a larger baking dish or cake pan. Pour an inch of water into the larger pan. Carefully transfer the baking dish into the oven and bake for 40-45 minutes, or until the flan has set.

While the flan is baking, make the Parmesan sauce. Place a skillet over medium heat and add butter. When it melts completely, sprinkle in the flour and whisk to combine smoothly. Continue to whisk the mixture for 2 minutes.

Slowly pour in the milk while continuing to whisk briskly, to ensure the sauce is smooth with no lumps. Whisk in salt and Parmesan cheese. Reduce the heat to low and let the mixture simmer, stirring occasionally, for 8 minutes. Remove the mixture to a large mixing bowl and set aside until the flan is ready.

Remove the flan from the oven and allow to cool for 30 minutes. Top with some of the Parmesan sauce and serve.

Cheesy Pasta Pie
(Torta di Bucatini)
ITALY

This dish is typically one of those clean-out-the-fridge things, sort of like a frittata or a super weird smoothie. So, if you happen to have this specific list of items hanging around the ol' icebox, *great!* Otherwise, just trust me and go to the market. This combination of flavors and textures is brilliant. My last smoothie, not so much.

—Greg

TOTAL TIME: 1 hour, 15 minutes
CHARACTER: Main, Side
VESSEL: 9 x 13 inch baking dish, or equivalent
SERVES: 10–12

4 qt water
2 Tbsp + 1 tsp salt, divided
12 oz dry bucatini or spaghetti pasta
3 large eggs
½ cup light cream or half-and-half
¼ cup + 1 Tbsp extra-virgin olive oil, divided
1 cup Pecorino cheese, grated or shredded, divided
1 cup Asiago cheese, shredded, divided
1 Tbsp dried oregano
1 clove garlic, minced
1 tsp ground black pepper
1 medium red bell pepper, roasted, peeled, minced
Tomato sauce for serving

Preheat the oven to 400°F. In a large pot, bring water to a rolling boil over high heat. Once boiling, add 2 tablespoons of salt and pasta. Cook for 10 minutes, occasionally stirring to ensure the pasta does not stick to the pot. Drain the pasta in a colander, spray with cold water to stop the pasta from cooking further, and set aside while you prepare the other ingredients.

In a large mixing bowl, combine the eggs, cream, ¼ cup of the olive oil, ½ cup each of the cheeses, oregano, garlic, black pepper, and remaining 1 teaspoon of salt, and whisk until combined. To the bowl, add the spaghetti and roasted pepper. Using two forks like salad tongs, toss the mixture together, evenly distributing the pasta with all the good bits.

Add 1 tablespoon of olive oil to baking dish to coat the bottom and sides. Pour pasta mixture into the baking dish and press the top with the back of a spoon to level the surface and evenly distribute the liquid. Top the pasta mixture with the remaining cheese. Place the baking dish in the oven for 30-35 minutes or until the top is just beginning to brown.

This dish is best served at room temperature, but serving it hot is still delicious. The cooler the "pie" gets, the easier it is to cut into beautiful blocks and serve with tomato sauce.

Warm Barley Salad
(Insalata di Orzo)

ITALY

TOTAL TIME: 1 hour, 10 minutes
CHARACTER: Side
VESSEL: 10 inch cast iron skillet with a lid, 8 x 8 inch baking dish with a lid, or equivalent
SERVES: 6-8

> Sure, you can cook up some barley, toss it in a big bowl with the rest of the ingredients, and call that a salad. *Or,* you can bake it all together as a casserole and then it actually tastes like something.
>
> —Howie

2 cups water
1 cup pearled barley
1 tsp salt
1 tsp ground black pepper
1 cup cherry tomatoes, halved
1 cup kalamata (or other black) olives, pitted, halved
4 Tbsp extra-virgin olive oil, divided
½ cup basil leaves, roughly chopped

Preheat the oven to 375°F. In a microwave, kettle, or on the stovetop, boil the water. In a skillet or baking dish, stir together barley, salt, pepper, tomatoes, olives, and 2 tablespoons of the olive oil. Pour in boiling water and stir to combine.

Either wrap tightly with foil or place the lid on the vessel; transfer to the oven. Bake for 60 minutes. Remove from the oven, remove the cover, drizzle with the remaining 2 tablespoons of olive oil, sprinkle with basil, and serve.

Tuna Lasagna
(Lasagne al Tonno)
ITALY

TOTAL TIME: 1 hour, 15 minutes
CHARACTER: Main, Side
VESSEL: 9 x 13 inch baking dish, or equivalent
SERVES: 6-8

1 Tbsp extra-virgin olive oil
1 onion, diced
2 stalks celery
2 cloves garlic, minced
1 28-oz can of crushed or pureed tomatoes
½ cup Parmesan cheese, shredded or grated
1 cup green olives, pitted, halved
15 oz ricotta cheese
3 5-oz cans tuna in water, drained
1 Tbsp dried oregano
9 oz no-boil (oven-ready) lasagna noodles
4 cups mozzarella cheese, shredded

As Americans, we see a can of tuna and get pretty excited about tuna salad. Italians, on the other hand, consider a can of tuna and envision rich sauces, bold experiments, and exquisite recipes, including this luscious lasagna. In Italy, not only do they class up what they do with canned tuna, they actually class up canned tuna. Luxury brands are dedicated to improving it year after year. We should tear a page right out of their playbook. Just sayin'.

—Howie

Preheat the oven to 350°F. Place a skillet over medium heat. Add 1 tablespoon of olive oil. When the oil begins to shimmer, add the onion and celery and sauté for 6–8 minutes, until translucent. Add the garlic and sauté another 2 minutes. Carefully pour in the tomatoes, then stir in the Parmesan, olives, ricotta, tuna, and oregano. Reduce the heat to low and let the sauce simmer for 15 minutes.

In a baking dish, spread 1 cup of the sauce over the bottom. Over that, add a single layer of noodles. Add another cup of sauce, and sprinkle with ¾ cup of the mozzarella. Repeat three more times (noodles, sauce, cheese). If you find you have remaining ingredients for another layer, go for it! Top with any remaining cheese. Cover tightly with aluminum foil. Bake for 30 minutes.

Remove the lasagna from the oven, uncover, and return to oven for 10–15 minutes, or until top is lightly browned. Allow the lasagna to rest for 10 minutes before slicing and serving.

Creamy Blue Cheese Orzo
(Orzo Pasta al Forno con Gorgonzola)

ITALY

TOTAL TIME: 1 hour, 15 minutes
CHARACTER: Side
VESSEL: 8 x 8 inch baking dish, or equivalent
SERVES: 6–8

"Orzo" in Italian means barley, the grain. "Orzo" is also the name of a pasta shape—it looks like a big piece of rice. In Italy, if you're referring to the pasta, you say "orzo pasta." If you're referring to barley, you say "orzo." In English, we already have a word for barley—coincidentally, it's "barley." Having a separate word allows us to simply refer to "orzo pasta" as "orzo." Think of all the ink we've saved!

—Greg

3 qt water
1 lb dry orzo pasta
2 Tbsp + 1 tsp salt, divided
4 Tbsp (½ stick) butter
¼ cup flour
2 cup milk
1 tsp ground black pepper
1 cup Parmesan cheese, grated or shredded, divided
1 cup Gorgonzola or other crumbly blue cheese, crumbled
½ cup parsley, chopped
1 Tbsp extra-virgin olive oil

Preheat oven to 375°F.

In a large pot, bring water to a rolling boil over high heat. Add pasta and 2 tablespoons of salt. Cook for 10 minutes, stirring occasionally to ensure the pasta does not stick to the pot. Drain the pasta, and rinse with cold water to ensure the pasta does not overcook. Set aside.

Place a skillet over medium heat and add butter. When it melts completely, sprinkle in the flour and whisk to combine completely. Continue to whisk the mixture for 2 minutes. Slowly pour in the milk while continuing to whisk briskly, to ensure the sauce is smooth with no lumps. Stir in pepper, and the remaining 1 teaspoon of salt. Reduce the heat to low and let the mixture simmer, stirring occasionally for 6 minutes.

To the skillet, add ½ cup of the Parmesan and all the Gorgonzola. Melt the cheese into the sauce (some lumps of blue cheese is okay) and continue to simmer for an additional 2 minutes. Remove the mixture to a large mixing bowl. To the mixing bowl, stir in the parsley and the drained orzo.

Coat the bottom and sides of a baking dish with olive oil. Pour the mixing bowl contents into the baking dish and top with the remaining ½ cup of Parmesan. Transfer the baking dish to the oven and bake for 45–50 minutes, or until the top is golden.

Allow the casserole to cool for 10–15 minutes before serving heaping spoonfuls. Try to include some of the chewy top with every serving.

"Botched" Cornmeal Casserole
(Polenta Pasticciata)
ITALY

TOTAL TIME: 1 hour, 20 minutes
CHARACTER: Main, Side
VESSEL: 9 x 13 inch baking dish, or equivalent
SERVES: 6-8

I love polenta. The simplicity of smooth, creamy, golden cornmeal is an awesome foil for a typical topping like a Bolognese sauce, sautéed greens, or roasted meats. But, it's often fun to get funky with polenta and really *mess it up*. Why take something perfect as it is and cook up a recipe that literally *botches* it? Because sausage and cheese. That's why.

—Howie

3 cups water
¾ cup whole milk
1 tsp salt, divided
1 cup polenta or coarse cornmeal
1 cup Parmesan cheese, grated, divided
3 Tbsp butter, divided
1 onion, diced
1 lb pork sausage, raw, casings removed
8 oz Fontina cheese, sliced
½ cup parsley, chopped

Preheat oven to 350°F.

In a medium pot on the stove, bring water, milk, and ½ teaspoon salt to a boil. Reduce the heat and maintain a simmer. Slowly whisk the polenta into the liquid in a steady stream, being sure to whisk quickly to avoid any polenta lumps. Continue to whisk until the polenta begins to thicken, about 5-6 minutes. Remove from the heat, and using a spoon instead of a whisk, continue to stir the polenta until it is very thick, like thick porridge, about an additional 5-6 minutes. Stir in and incorporate 1 tablespoon of butter and ½ cup of Parmesan.

Using 1 tablespoon of butter, grease the bottom and sides of a baking dish. Pour half of the polenta into the baking dish and set aside to cool.

Place a skillet over medium-high heat. Add the remaining 1 tablespoon of butter. Once the butter has melted, add onion and ½ teaspoon of salt, and sauté until the onion is soft, about 4-6 minutes. Add sausage, breaking it into small pieces and continue to sauté until the sausage is browned, about 4-6 more minutes.

Gently distribute the sausage mixture atop the polenta layer in the baking dish and sprinkle with the remaining ½ cup of Parmesan. Place slices of Fontina cheese atop the sausage. On top of the cheese, scoop and smooth the remaining polenta in a single layer.

Transfer the baking dish to the oven and roast for 30 minutes or until the polenta at the top begins to brown slightly. Remove from the oven and allow the casserole to cool for 10-15 minutes. Garnish with parsley and serve slices of the "botched polenta" along with something saucy.

Ham and Cheese Bread Pudding

(Pain Perdu au Fromage et Jambon)

FRANCE

TOTAL TIME: 2 hours
CHARACTER: One Pot Meal, Main
VESSEL: 9 x 13 inch, deep 8 x 8 inch baking dish, or equivalent
SERVES: 6–8

5 cups (about 1 lb) crusty bread, cubed
12 oz Gruyère cheese, shredded
12 oz ham, diced or thin strips
4 Tbsp parsley, chopped
5 eggs
2 cups half-and-half or milk
¾ cup sour cream
1 Tbsp dry sherry
1 Tbsp dried thyme
1 tsp onion powder
1 tsp salt
1 tsp ground black pepper
3 Tbsp butter, melted

In France, *French toast* is referred to as "pain perdu," which translates to "lost bread." It's a popular way to revive stale or "lost" bread. You know what else got lost? The fact that "French toast" has nothing to do with France! It was popularized in the US in the mid-18th century by an Upstate New York innkeeper named Joseph *French*. Anyhow, here's a bread dish that's actually French.

—Howie

Preheat the oven to 425°F. In a large mixing bowl, toss the bread cubes with Gruyère, ham, and parsley. In another mixing bowl, whisk together remaining ingredients (except butter).

Coat the bottom and sides of a baking dish with melted butter; reserve the rest. Evenly pour the bread mixture into the baking dish. Be sure you have one even layer with a flat top (no bread hills).

Slowly pour the egg mixture evenly over the bread mixture, being sure that some of the liquid reaches most, if not all, of the bread. Use the back of a wooden spoon, a clean hand, or spatula, to compress the whole mixture to ensure that the liquid is evenly distributed. Cover the baking dish and allow it to rest, undisturbed, for one hour.

Remove the plastic wrap, drizzle with the remaining butter, and transfer the baking dish to the center rack of the oven. Bake for 40–45 minutes, or until the top begins to get brown and crusty.

Remove the casserole from the oven and allow it to cool for 10 minutes before slicing and serving.

Cheesy Bread in Broth
(Panade au Raclette)
FRANCE

TOTAL TIME: 1 hour, 55 minutes
CHARACTER: One Pot Meal, Main
VESSEL: 11 x 13 inch baking dish, or equivalent
SERVES: 6-8

As Americans, we know how to use leftover bread . . . Or, do we? Bread crumbs and croutons, check! Well, of course we also make the best Thanksgiving "stuffing!" That covers everything, right? Nope. The rest of the world opens the door a bit further? How about the Italian solutions, Tuscan ribollita soup or panzanella salad? The Germans offer up the brilliant strata. Then, what may be the prince of old bread—have you considered a succulent, vegetable-laden French panade? It's like "stuffing" on hydraulics.

—Howie

3½ cups chicken or vegetable broth
2 Tbsp extra-virgin olive oil
2 large onions, sliced thinly
1½ lb crusty sourdough bread, cut into ½ inch slices
12 oz baby spinach
2 cloves garlic, minced
¼ cup white wine
1 tsp dried thyme
1 tsp salt
½ tsp ground black pepper
2 lb grape or cherry tomatoes, some halved, some whole, divided
12 oz raclette or Gruyère cheese, shredded

Preheat the oven to 400°F. In a small pot on the stove, bring the broth to a boil, reduce the heat, and keep warm while you prepare the other ingredients.

Place a skillet over medium-low heat. Add half the olive oil. Once the oil begins to shimmer, add the onions and sauté them until they are very soft and caramelized, about 25-30 minutes. Stir the onions every few minutes to assure even cooking. While the onions are cooking, toast the bread slices in a toaster or in the oven on a sheet pan for 10-12 minutes. You know what toast looks like.

continued on page 208

Raise the heat under the onions to medium-high and add the spinach, garlic, wine, thyme, salt, and pepper to the skillet. Continue to sauté the mixture until the spinach has wilted, and the liquid is almost completely gone, about 5-7 minutes. Turn off the heat.

Coat the bottom and sides of a baking dish with the remaining 1 tablespoon of olive oil.

Place a layer of the toast at the bottom of the baking dish. Fit the toast in a single layer as best you can. Then, spread half of the onion mixture atop the toast, followed by a third of the tomatoes and half of the cheese. Place another layer of toast atop the cheese. Repeat onion mixture, a third of the tomatoes, and second half of the cheese. Place the final layer of toast atop the cheese.

Slowly pour the broth evenly over the bread mixture, being sure that some of the liquid reaches most, if not all, of the bread. Use the back of a wooden spoon or spatula to compress the whole mixture to ensure that the liquid is evenly distributed.

Cover the baking dish tightly with foil and transfer to the center rack of the oven. Bake for 50 minutes. Uncover the baking dish and continue to bake for 10-15 minutes or until the top begins to brown and get crusty.

Remove the panade from the oven and allow it to cool for 10 minutes before topping with remaining tomatoes, scooping, and serving.

Eggplant Tomato Stack
(Imam Bayildi)
TURKEY

TOTAL TIME: 2 hours
CHARACTER: Side
VESSEL: 9 x 13 inch baking dish, or equivalent
SERVES: 6-8

3 medium eggplants, cut into ¼-inch rounds
2 Tbsp + 1 tsp salt
⅓ cup extra-virgin olive oil, divided
1 large white onion, diced
3 cloves garlic, minced
1 tsp ancho or other chile powder
1 28-oz can crushed tomatoes
½ tsp cinnamon
1 tsp sugar
1 Tbsp dried oregano
½ cup parsley, chopped, divided

If you speak Turkish (and who doesn't), you might have noticed the odd name for this dish. The story goes like this—there's this *imam* of a mosque, you know, the guy who leads the prayers? So, one day his wife makes this dish for him and he faints, or *bayildi*. I can see why. The dish is outstanding. It may well knock your socks off, and as such, there's some small chance that you too will go down in a heap. I'm not guaranteeing that you'll faint, but, just to be safe, I'd recommend that you line your dining room with pillows.

—Greg

Preheat the oven to 400°F.

Line a baking sheet with paper towels and lay the eggplant slices flat. Salt both sides of the slices using 2 tablespoons of the salt. If you run out of room on the sheet pan, place another layer of paper towels atop the eggplant and create another layer of salted slices.

While the eggplant is losing some of its water, prepare the tomato sauce. Place a skillet over medium heat. Add 2 tablespoons of olive oil. When the oil begins to shimmer, add onion and remaining 1 teaspoon of salt to the skillet and sauté for 6-8 minutes, or until the onion begins to become translucent. Add garlic and chile powder and continue to sauté for an additional minute. Pour in the crushed tomatoes, and stir in cinnamon, sugar, oregano, and ¼ cup of parsley. Reduce the heat to low and allow this mixture to simmer for 15 minutes.

continued on page 211

Pat the eggplant slices dry with fresh paper towels. Place eggplant slices on sheet pans and brush the tops with the remaining olive oil. Transfer the sheet pan to the oven and roast for 20–25 minutes or until the eggplant has softened and begun to turn brown. Remove the eggplant from the oven and lower the temperature to 350°F.

In a baking dish, pour 1 cup of the tomato sauce on the bottom. Create a layer of eggplant slices, and top it with another 1 cup of the tomato sauce. Then, add another layer of eggplant, 1 cup of the tomato sauce, eggplant, and finally the last 1 cup of tomato sauce. Cover the baking dish tightly with aluminum foil, and roast in the oven for 50 minutes.

Remove from the oven and allow the casserole to cool for 15 minutes. Remove the foil, and sprinkle with the remaining ¼ cup of parsley before serving up hot slices.

Creamy Herbed Potatoes
(Gratin Dauphinois)

FRANCE

TOTAL TIME: 1 hour, 45 minutes
CHARACTER: Side
VESSEL: 9 x 13 inch baking dish, or equivalent
SERVES: 6-8

- 3 Tbsp unsalted butter, divided
- 5-6 (about 2½-3 lb) russet potatoes, peeled, sliced ⅛-inch thick (a mandoline helps)
- 3 tsp fresh thyme leaves, divided
- 3 cups heavy cream
- 2 tsp salt
- 1 tsp ground black pepper
- 1 tsp garlic powder

These days, you can pop open a Web browser and find "gratin" recipes for everything from Brussels sprouts to corn chips with crab. Nope, not kidding. Gratin potatoes seems like a throwback, eh? There is a reason that this gorgeous dish is still world champ: It makes *physical* culinary sense. The potatoes are giving up their starch at the same rate that the cream is able to absorb it, resulting in an endlessly creamy bite. You can have your un-vetted internet search results and corn chips. I'll take this classic, any day of the week.

—Howie

Preheat the oven to 350°F. Coat the bottom and sides of a baking dish with 1 tablespoon of butter.

Form a bottom layer in the baking dish using a third of the potato slices, overlapping them like shingles, followed by 1 teaspoon of thyme. Repeat with another layer of potato slices and 1 teaspoon of thyme. Place one last layer of the remaining potato on top.

In a medium mixing bowl, whisk together remaining ingredients except the thyme and butter. Slowly pour the cream mixture over the potatoes, giving it some time to fall to the bottom of the baking dish and surround its contents. Sprinkle 1 teaspoon of thyme across the top, and dot with pinches of the remaining butter.

Cover the dish tightly with aluminum foil, transfer to the oven, and bake for 1 hour. Remove from the oven, discard the foil, and return to the oven uncovered, for an additional 10-15 minutes or until the top begins to brown.

Remove the gratin from the oven and allow it to cool for 10-15 minutes. Serve in loving, heaping spoonfuls.

Nice Squash and Eggplant Casserole

(Ratatouille Niçoise)

FRANCE

TOTAL TIME: 3 hours, 45 minutes
CHARACTER: Side
VESSEL: 9 x 13 inch baking dish, or equivalent
SERVES: 8-10

1 large eggplant, diced
3 tsp salt, divided
4 medium tomatoes, diced
8 Tbsp extra-virgin olive oil, divided
2 large onions, diced
2 green bell peppers, diced
2 red bell peppers, diced
3 cloves garlic, minced
3 medium zucchini, diced
3 medium yellow squash, diced
1 Tbsp dried oregano
1 Tbsp dried basil
1 Tbsp dried thyme
¼ cup fresh basil, roughly chopped

There's this cartoon movie about a rat who knows his way around a kitchen and figures out how to "drive" a bumbling human into creating culinary masterpieces. The climax of the movie sees our rodent friend crafting a classed-up version of this peasant dish for a cantankerous restaurant critic who upon taking one bite is sent reeling back to his childhood. Where we can't promise life-altering flashbacks, we can briefly transport you to Provence.

—Greg

In a large colander over a plate, combine eggplant and ½ teaspoon of salt. In a separate colander over a plate, combine tomatoes and ½ teaspoon of salt. Allow these to rest for at least 30 minutes while you prepare the remainder of ingredients.

Preheat the oven to 300°F.

Place a large skillet (or even better, a wok) over medium heat. Add 2 tablespoons of olive oil. When the oil shimmers, add onions and 1 teaspoon of salt, and sauté for 4-6 minutes, or until the onions are limp. Add the peppers and continue to sauté for an additional 4-6 minutes, or until the peppers are soft. Add the tomatoes and garlic and continue to sauté for 4-6 minutes, or until the tomatoes are soft. Transfer the mixture to a large mixing bowl and wipe out the skillet.

Add 6 tablespoons of olive oil to the skillet. When the oil shimmers, add eggplant, zucchini, yellow squash, and remaining 1 teaspoon of salt, and sauté until the outsides of the vegetables have softened a bit, about 6-8 minutes.

In the same large mixing bowl with the onions, peppers, and tomatoes, mix in the eggplant and squashes, along with the dried herbs. Pour the mixing bowl contents into a baking dish, cover tightly with aluminum foil, and roast in the oven for 3 hours. Remove the ratatouille from the oven, garnish with fresh basil, and serve hot or warm.

Asia

Creamy Bacon Rice Casserole
(Bēkon Doria)
JAPAN

TOTAL TIME: 1 hour
CHARACTER: One Pot Meal, Main
VESSEL: 8 x 8 inch baking dish, or equivalent
SERVES: 6-8

There comes a time in everyone's food life when you run into a dish that is so *wrong* that it's *right*. There's little about this casserole that makes any sense. Curried rice with a béchamel sauce? Cooked avocado, Italian sausage, soy sauce, and mozzarella? Long ago, the Japanese gleaned this dish idea from a Italian family named Doria—perhaps inspired by lasagna? Then, the Japanese culinary machine went into overdrive. Just make it. Allow complete and utter surprise to overwhelm your taste buds.

—Howie

WHITE SAUCE:

4 Tbsp (½ stick) butter
¼ cup flour
2 cups milk
½ tsp salt
¼ tsp ground black pepper
1 ripe avocado, peeled, pitted, diced

MEAT FILLING:

½ lb bacon, diced
½ lb Italian sausage, casings removed
2 tsp sweet curry powder

RICE FILLING:

½ cup carrot, shredded
3 scallions, thinly sliced
2 cups cooked white rice
2 cloves garlic, minced
3 Tbsp soy sauce

CASSEROLE:

1 Tbsp extra-virgin olive oil
1 cup mozzarella cheese, shredded

continued on page 220

Preheat the oven to 375°F.

To make the white sauce, place a skillet over medium heat and add butter. When it has melted, sprinkle in the flour and whisk it to combine completely. Continue to whisk and cook the mixture for 2 minutes. Slowly pour in the milk while continuing to whisk briskly, to ensure the sauce is smooth with no lumps. Stir in salt and pepper. Reduce the heat to low and let the mixture simmer, stirring occasionally, for 8 minutes. Fold in the diced avocado and set aside.

To make the meat filling, place a separate skillet over medium heat. Add the bacon and sauté until just browned, about 6-8 minutes. Add sausage and continue to sauté for another 8 minutes, or until the sausage is browned. Be sure to break up the sausage into small bits as you sauté. Add curry powder and stir to combine. Using a slotted spoon, transfer the meats from the skillet to a bowl, leaving some of the flavored oil behind, and set aside.

To make the rice filling, place the same skillet over medium heat. Add the carrot and sauté for 4-5 minutes, or until the carrot is soft. Add the scallions and continue to sauté for an additional 3 minutes. Add the rice and garlic, and continue to sauté for an additional 5 minutes, or until the rice has warmed through and is light brown in color. Stir in the soy sauce.

To assemble the casserole, spread olive oil across the bottom and sides of a baking dish. Place the fried rice at the bottom and flatten into a consistent layer with the back of a spoon or a clean hand. Scatter the meat filling atop the rice, then evenly pour the white sauce over the top. Sprinkle with mozzarella cheese.

Transfer the baking dish into the oven and bake for 25-30 minutes, or until the mozzarella cheese is completely melted and just beginning to brown. Remove the doria from the oven, and serve hot, directly into intrigued diners' bowls.

Eggplant Clay Pot
(Qiezi Bao)
CHINA

TOTAL TIME: 1 hour, 40 minutes
CHARACTER: Side
VESSEL: 8 inch cast iron skillet with a lid, or other oven-safe skillet with a lid
SERVES: 4–6

Greg and I were in the middle of Hunan Province hiking up this craggy mountain in a national park. It turns out, this is where the movie *Avatar* was filmed. Big, spiky karst formations with tight, cliff-hugging footpaths winding up tall, thin peaks. We chose one of the less popular paths up to the top, to avoid big crowds. Dumb move. After reaching the top, and starting down, We heard *crrraaaaccckkk*, and as we look across the narrow valley, we watch the face of one of these cliffs shear off and fall 1,000 feet into a cloud of its former self. *Wait. Another crack! Run!* Anyway, that night, we had this nerve-restoring dish for dinner.

—Howie

1 oz dried shiitake mushrooms, diced
2 cups boiling water
2 large Italian or globe eggplants
1 Tbsp vegetable oil
2 scallions, thinly sliced
1 clove garlic, minced
½ jalapeño pepper, stemmed, seeded, minced
2 Tbsp Chinese broad bean paste, or other Asian chile paste
1 Tbsp cornstarch
2 Tbsp soy sauce
1 tsp sugar
1 tsp sesame oil
½ cup cilantro, chopped

Preheat the oven to 375°F. In a heatproof bowl, combine mushrooms and boiling water, stir, and set aside.

Using the tip of a sharp knife, prick 5-10 slits in the skin of the eggplants, and place directly on the oven rack. Roast for one hour, flipping them halfway through. Remove the eggplants from the oven, place them on a plate, and allow them to cool while you prepare the remainder of ingredients. Lower the oven to 300°F.

continued on page 223

Drain the mushrooms, keeping 1 cup of the soaking liquid. Place oil in a skillet over medium-high heat. When the oil begins to shimmer, add scallions, garlic, and jalapeño, and sauté for 2 minutes. Add mushrooms, broad bean or chile paste, and continue to sauté for an additional minute. In a small mixing bowl, whisk the reserved mushroom liquid with cornstarch, and pour this mixture into the skillet, along with soy sauce and sugar. Bring the mixture to a boil, and remove from the heat.

Transfer the eggplants to a cutting board. Slice them in half lengthwise and scoop out the roasted flesh, discarding the skins. Chop the eggplant flesh into bite-sized pieces. Add eggplant to the skillet and give everything a good mix. Cover the skillet and transfer to the oven for 25-30 minutes.

Remove the skillet from the oven, uncover, drizzle with sesame oil, and top with cilantro. Serve with steamed white rice.

“Water-Boiled” Fish
(Shuizhu Yu)
CHINA

TOTAL TIME: 40 minutes
CHARACTER: Main
VESSEL: 10 inch cast iron skillet, or other oven-safe skillet
SERVES: 6-8

1½ lb tilapia fillets, cut into 2-inch pieces
1 egg white
1 Tbsp cornstarch
1 tsp salt
3 Tbsp vegetable oil
2 scallions, thinly sliced, white and green parts separated
4 cloves garlic, minced
1 inch ginger, minced
3 Tbsp Chinese broad bean paste, or other medium chile paste
3 Tbsp soy sauce
3 cups water
¼ tsp ground cinnamon
2 tsp dried red chile flakes
½ head Napa cabbage, shredded
1 Tbsp sesame seeds (optional)

Howie and I were in rural Sichuan Province hiking in the bamboo sea. This is where they filmed some of the coolest tree-top fighting scenes in *Crouching Tiger, Hidden Dragon*. As usual, we took the path least traveled and wound our way up to a beautiful waterfall. Thinking we were following the same general path as the main trail, we got lost. As it turns out, bamboo pretty much all looks the same up close . . . and from far away. With the help of a machete-wielding mushroom poacher, we made it out alive. Anyway, that night, since we'd had enough of bamboo shoots, we had this Sichuan dish for dinner.

—Greg

Preheat the oven to 350°F.

In a mixing bowl, combine fish pieces with egg white, cornstarch, and salt. Be sure the cornstarch gets fully absorbed into the marinade.

Place a skillet over medium heat, and add the oil. When the oil begins to shimmer, add the white parts of the scallions, garlic, and ginger and sauté for 3-4 minutes, or until the scallions start to become translucent. Add the broad bean or chile paste and sauté for an additional 2 minutes. Add soy sauce, water, cinnamon, and chile flakes, and stir well. Bring the mixture to a boil and turn off the heat.

Carefully distribute the marinated fish pieces into the skillet, stir them into the mix, and transfer the skillet to the oven and braise for 20-25 minutes, or until the fish is cooked through.

Place the shredded cabbage at the bottom of a serving bowl or platter with a tall rim. Remove the skillet from the oven. Carefully transfer the skillet contents into the serving vessel atop the cabbage. Top with scallion greens and sprinkle with sesame seeds, if using. Serve with steamed white rice.

Savory Egg Broth Custard
(Jidan Geng)

CHINA

TOTAL TIME: 40 minutes
CHARACTER: Side
VESSEL: 8 x 8 inch baking dish, or equivalent
SERVES: 6-8

- 8 eggs
- 1 tsp salt
- 2 tsp soy sauce
- 2 cups vegetable or chicken broth
- 2 tsp vegetable oil
- 3 scallions, thinly sliced

Greg and I were in rural Yunnan Province traipsing about enormous valleys of terraced rice fields. It's as beautiful as you imagine. We had a great time talking with locals and learning about rice cultivation. Then it came time to hire a car to take us the nine hours back to civilization. That being said, China + cliffs + one-lane roads + 80 mph + hairpin turns = White-knuckled Howie, holding on for dear life. Greg responded differently, laughing and *even falling asleep* along the way. Anyway, that night we had this dish for a well-deserved and calming dinner.

—Howie

Preheat the oven to 350°F.

In a blender or food processor, combine eggs, salt, soy sauce, broth, and oil. Blend until very smooth. Be sure the egg whites are no longer visible. If you think you can accomplish this with a bowl and a whisk, go for it.

Pour the mixture into a baking dish and scatter scallions across the top.

Place the baking dish into a larger baking dish or cake pan. Fill the larger pan with an inch of boiling water. Cover and carefully transfer the set of baking vessels into the oven. Bake for 45-50 minutes, or until the custard is set in the middle. Carefully remove the cover and test with a little jiggle. If it is not yet set, leave it in the oven for increments of ONE additional minute. Jiggle again.

Serve scoops with some steamed rice.

Lion's Head Casserole
(Shizi Tou)
CHINA

TOTAL TIME: 1 hour
CHARACTER: One Pot Meal, Main
VESSEL: 9 x 13 inch baking dish, or equivalent
SERVES: 4–6

This is an adaptation of a classic Shanghai dish, lion's head meatballs. The name comes from its original format with a hearty pork meatball surrounded by leafy cabbage, or, the "mane." This casserole-ization maintains the juicy spirit of the dish and simply forms layers out of the three savory stars of the show: rice noodles, cabbage, and of course, the meat. Hao Chi!

—Howie

MEAT MIXTURE:

1 lb ground pork (not lean)
6 oz firm tofu, crumbled
4 water chestnuts, minced
1 Tbsp Shaoxing wine, or dry sherry
1 Tbsp sesame oil
2 cloves garlic, minced
1 Tbsp ginger, minced
3 scallions, thinly sliced
2 Tbsp soy sauce
2 large eggs
1 tsp salt
½ tsp sugar
1 Tbsp water
8 oz (*not* jumbo lump) crab meat

CASSEROLE:

4 oz dry rice noodles, uncooked, roughly broken into 2-inch segments
6 oz (about 4 medium heads) baby bok choy
2 cups chicken broth
2 scallions, thinly sliced

Preheat the oven to 350°F. In a large mixing bowl, thoroughly combine all the meat mixture ingredients, aside from the crab meat. Fold in the crab meat, trying to keep bigger pieces from falling apart.

In a baking dish, place the rice noodle segments, and top with an even layer of the cabbage. Gently spread the meat mixture atop the cabbage. It helps to form thin patties of the meat with one's hands before placing atop the cabbage. Once you *mostly* cover the cabbage with meat mixture, use a wet hand to smooth the top over and fill in any gaps. BUT, leave a small opening at one corner of the baking dish.

Slowly pour warmed-up chicken broth into the corner opening, being sure not to disturb the meat layer. Then, carefully close the gap, pushing some of the meat mixture to close it up. Transfer the baking dish into the oven and roast for 35 minutes.

Remove the casserole from the oven, top with scallions, and serve hot, being sure to include some meat, cabbage, and noodles with each serving.

Hainan Chicken Rice
(Hainan Ji Fan)
CHINA/SINGAPORE

TOTAL TIME: 1 hour, 40 minutes
CHARACTER: Main
VESSEL: 9 x 13 inch baking dish, or equivalent
SERVES: 4–6

CASSEROLE:

3 lb (about 2 large) split chicken breasts, bone-in, skin on
3 Tbsp soy sauce
3 Tbsp toasted sesame oil
2 cups jasmine or other long grain rice, uncooked
7 scallions, white parts left whole, green parts thinly sliced, divided
3 inches ginger, cut into long, flat slices
3½ cups chicken broth

DIPPING PASTE:

1-2 Tbsp dried red chile flakes, to taste
1 head (about 10 cloves) garlic, peeled
2 inches ginger, peeled
2 tsp rice vinegar
2 tsp sugar
3 Tbsp lime juice (about 1 large lime)
3 Tbsp chicken broth
1 pinch salt

Howie and I were on Hainan Island in the South China Sea. With the sweet ocean breezes and overall tropical feel of this place, it took a real jolt to remind us that it's still China. We decided to get crafty, dig a pit in the sand, and make the famous luau dish, kalua pork, for lunch with local friends. Here's me with a metal shovel and the first pit I dig, *bam*, I hit power cables. Welcome back to China. Anyway, after losing interest in lunch that day, this is a dish we had for dinner.

—Greg

In a large mixing bowl, coat chicken with soy sauce and sesame oil and allow it to marinate for at least 30 minutes. Flip the chicken every few minutes to ensure even coating.

Preheat the oven to 375°F. In a baking dish, place uncooked rice across the bottom. Atop the rice, evenly distribute the whole scallion whites and ginger slices. Atop the scallions and ginger, place the marinated chicken, skin-side up. Discard the marinade.

Carefully pour chicken broth around the chicken, being sure not to disturb the rice layer and keeping the scallions and ginger pinned underneath the chicken. Tightly cover the baking dish with aluminum foil and transfer to the oven. Roast for 35 minutes. Remove the chicken rice from the oven and allow it to rest, covered, on the counter or stovetop for 15 minutes, undisturbed.

While the chicken rice is resting, make the dipping paste. Combine all paste ingredients in the bowl of a food processor and purée. Remove foil from the top of the chicken rice. Before serving, transfer chicken to a cutting board. Remove the scallion whites and ginger pieces from the rice. Chop the chicken into several pieces before placing back atop the rice, sprinkling with sliced scallion greens and serving alongside the spicy dipping paste.

Spicy Kimchi Tofu Pot
(Sundubu Jjigae)
SOUTH KOREA

TOTAL TIME: 1 hour, 10 minutes
CHARACTER: Main, Side
VESSEL: 10 inch cast iron skillet, or other oven-safe skillet
SERVES: 4-6

When I moved to China in 1996, I was not very good at travel arrangements. I booked my flight to Shanghai with the nine-hour layover in Seoul, South Korea. Those hours in the airport faded away when I met my first jjigae! Then, my second. Okay, there was a third in there, too. Nine hours, people! This dish is almost literally *burned* into my memory. My introduction to Korean cuisine was a spicy one indeed, and pretty darned representative.

—Howie

2 Tbsp Korean chile powder or dried red pepper flakes
2 Tbsp sesame oil
2 Tbsp soy sauce
1 Tbsp vegetable oil
3 slices bacon, diced (optional)
3 cloves garlic, minced
4 scallions, white and green parts separated, thinly sliced
1 jalapeño pepper, minced
2 cups prepared kimchi, roughly chopped
1 tsp salt
1 tsp sugar
2 cups prepared dashi or vegetable broth
2 lb silken tofu
4 eggs

Preheat the oven to 375°F. In a small mixing bowl, combine chile powder or red pepper flakes with sesame oil and soy sauce, and set aside.

Place a skillet over medium heat. Add vegetable oil. When the oil begins to shimmer, add bacon (if using) and sauté until browned, about 6-8 minutes. Add garlic, the white parts of the scallions, jalapeño, and kimchi, and continue to sauté for 4 minutes. Add salt, sugar, dashi or broth, and bring to a boil. Turn off the heat.

Crumble silken tofu into the skillet and stir to evenly distribute. Be sure to keep some larger pieces of tofu intact. Carefully transfer the skillet into the oven and braise for 35-40 minutes, or until the tofu begins to absorb red liquid. Remove the baking dish from the oven.

Sprinkle the chile soy mixture across the top of the jjigae. Crack the eggs neatly and evenly across the top. Return the skillet to the oven and bake for another 10–12 minutes, until egg whites are set and the yolks are still runny. Top with scallion greens and serve immediately with white rice and a smile.

Sausage Shrimp Rice Pot
(Bozai Fan)
HONG KONG

TOTAL TIME: 1 hour, 20 minutes
CHARACTER: One Pot Meal
VESSEL: 10 inch cast iron skillet with a lid, or other oven-safe skillet with a lid
SERVES: 4–6

1¾ cups water + more for soaking rice
1 oz dried shiitake mushrooms, diced
1 lb chicken thighs, skinless, boneless, diced
3 Tbsp soy sauce, divided
½ tsp black pepper
1 tsp sesame oil
1 Tbsp ginger, minced
1 clove garlic, minced
1 cup jasmine or other long grain rice, uncooked
1 Tbsp vegetable oil
2 scallions, thinly sliced, divided into greener and whiter parts
6 oz (2 small) Chinese lapchang or other cured sausage, diced

> My wife, Jessica, and I were in Guangzhou, China, just across the straits from Hong Kong. This was her first trip to China, and I was very excited to share this magical cuisine with her, finally! After a very long set of flights, which were terribly planned, we arrived into our hotel at 1:30 a.m. Much to my chagrin, the only food option in the neighborhood had some golden arches flying above the door. *Not-so-happy-meal!* The next day at lunch, I declared it to be our *first meal* in China. This dish is one highlight of that meal.
>
> —Howie

Preheat the oven to 375°F. Boil 1¾ cups water in the microwave or on the stove top. In a heatproof mixing bowl, combine the boiled water with dried mushrooms. Allow the mushrooms to rehydrate for 30 minutes.

In a separate mixing bowl, combine chicken, soy sauce, pepper, sesame oil, ginger, and garlic. Allow the chicken to marinate for 30 minutes. In the skillet that will go in the oven, soak the rice in cold water.

Drain the mushrooms and reserve the soaking liquid.

Place a separate skillet over medium-high heat. Add the oil. When the oil begins to shimmer, add the white parts of scallions, mushrooms, and sausage, and sauté for 3-4 minutes or until the scallions turn translucent.

Carefully pour off the soaking water from the rice in the oven skillet. Transfer scallions, mushrooms, and sausage from the other skillet to top the rice. Then, place the marinated chicken into the skillet, also above the rice. Carefully pour the reserved mushroom soaking liquid into the skillet, being sure not to disturb the rice at the bottom.

Bring the skillet to a boil over high heat. Cover and transfer the skillet to the oven for 25 minutes.

Remove the skillet from the oven. Allow the rice pot to rest, covered, for 15 minutes. Remove the lid, garnish with scallion greens, and serve directly to bowls, being sure to include all the good bits.

Shrimp Kettle Rice
(Kamameshi)
JAPAN

TOTAL TIME: 1 hour, 30 minutes
CHARACTER: One Pot Meal
VESSEL: 10 inch cast iron skillet with a lid, or other oven-safe skillet with a lid
SERVES: 4–6

I once had the opportunity to spend 72 hours in Tokyo. It's a gigantic city with more culinary options than should be presented to any human. This being the case, 72 hours was a ridiculously short time and I had to limit myself to brief bouts of sleep, followed by long binges of eating. I was not unsuccessful, but I was a tad tired and very, very full. Of course, I gorged on what you may find typical; your sushi, your tempura, your ramen. But, this gem stood out. I had met the most famous casserole you've never heard of.

—Howie

- 1¾ cup prepared dashi or vegetable broth
- 1 oz dried shiitake mushrooms, diced
- 1 lb shrimp, peeled, deveined, diced
- 4 Tbsp soy sauce, divided
- 1 cup jasmine or other long grain rice, uncooked
- 1 Tbsp mirin (or dry sherry)
- 1 Tbsp sake (or dry white wine)
- 4 scallions, sliced thinly, divided into greener and whiter parts
- 4 oz carrot, shredded
- 7 oz tofu (baked or extra firm), diced
- 1 tsp ground black pepper

Preheat the oven to 375°F.

Boil broth. In a heatproof mixing bowl, combine the broth with dried mushrooms. Allow the mushrooms to rehydrate for 30 minutes. In a separate mixing bowl, combine shrimp and half the soy sauce. Rinse the rice until the water runs clear and drain. Set aside the rinsed rice, marinating shrimp, and rehydrating mushrooms.

In a skillet, combine 2 Tbsp soy sauce and the remaining ingredients, except for the scallion greens. Once the mushrooms have rehydrated, pour the mushrooms and accompanying broth into the skillet and stir. Bring the mixture to a boil over high heat, add the rice, and stir to distribute evenly. Cover and transfer the skillet to the oven for 25 minutes.

Remove from the oven, carefully remove the cover, and distribute the marinated shrimp across the top of the skillet. Replace the cover, and transfer back to the oven for 10 more minutes.

Remove the skillet from the oven. Allow the kamameshi to rest, covered, for 15 minutes. Remove the lid, garnish with scallion greens, and serve directly to bowls.

Braised Catfish Pot
(Ca Bong Lau Kho To)
VIETNAM

TOTAL TIME: 50 minutes
CHARACTER: Main
VESSEL: 10 inch cast iron skillet, or other oven-safe skillet
SERVES: 6-8

1 Tbsp vegetable oil
1 small red onion, thinly sliced
2 cloves garlic, minced
4 Tbsp soy sauce
1 Tbsp fish sauce
1 tsp ground black pepper
1 Tbsp sugar
2 Thai bird chiles or 1 jalapeño, thinly sliced
1½ lb (about 3-4) catfish fillets, cut into 2-inch pieces
6 oz coconut water
6 oz sparkling water
1 scallion, thinly sliced

> I thoroughly enjoy when a fish dish surprises the taste buds. *Wait, there's catfish, a very fishy fish, and fish sauce? How is this dish not fishy?* Vietnamese alchemy, of course! This is not to say that you do not taste the catfish, and it certainly retains its meaty texture, but when combined with the deeply caramelized onion, punchy chiles, uniquely tropical coconut water, and all the supporting players, it becomes the star catfish its parents always thought it could be. Then, it gets eaten.
>
> —Howie

Preheat the oven to 350°F.

Place a skillet over medium-high heat, and add the oil. When the oil begins to shimmer, add onion and sauté for 6-8 minutes or until it begins to brown. Add garlic and continue to sauté for an additional minute. Add soy sauce, fish sauce, black pepper, sugar, and chiles, and mix well.

Place the catfish pieces atop the mixture in the skillet and allow them to cook on the bottom side for 2 minutes before flipping to cook the other side for an additional minute.

Pour the coconut water and sparkling water into the skillet. Bring the mixture to a boil, and remove from the heat. Transfer the uncovered skillet to the oven and braise for 25-30 minutes, or until the liquid reduces to about half, and the catfish is exposed and has darkened in color.

Remove the vessel from the oven, and top with scallion slices. Serve with steamed white rice.

Zesty Vegetable Rice
(Channai Veg Biryani)

INDIA

TOTAL TIME: 1 hour, 45 minutes
CHARACTER: One Pot Meal, Side
VESSEL: 11 x 15 inch baking dish, or equivalent
SERVES: 8-10

I used to work with a kindly Indian gentleman by the name of Srinivas from Channai. One day he brought some of his wife's biryani rice to work and asked me to try it out at home. I shared this incredible dish with my wife and she and I agreed that we couldn't handle it without a good dollop of sour cream, a full glass of milk, and some bread! *Hot, hot, hot!* When I told Srinivas the next day, he began to chuckle. He smarted, *That is what we prepare for our two-year-old!* The following three recipes are dedicated to Srinivas. They highlight the incredible ability of Indian cooks to take very similar ingredients and generate three quite different culinary experiences. I promise, they are not nearly as hot as Srinivas, his wife, or their *toddler* would have liked, but they still pack quite a kick.

—Howie

- 1½ cups basmati or other long grain rice, uncooked
- 5 cups water, divided
- 4 cloves garlic
- 2 inches fresh ginger, peeled
- 1 lemon, juiced
- 1 cup Greek-style yogurt
- ¼ cup heavy cream
- 3 Tbsp ghee or clarified butter
- 2 large onions
- 1 tsp ground cumin
- 1 tsp ground cayenne or other chile pepper
- 1 tsp smoked paprika
- 1 tsp ground black pepper
- ½ tsp garam masala or other curry powder
- ½ tsp turmeric powder
- 1 (about ½ lb) large russet potato, peeled, diced
- ½ head cauliflower, cut into florets
- 8 oz (about 2 large) carrots, diced
- 1½ tsp salt, divided
- 1 large tomato, diced
- 1 jalapeño pepper, stemmed, diced (with seeds)
- ½ lb French beans, haricot verts, or green beans, diced
- ½ cup fresh green peas
- ½ cup cilantro leaves, roughly chopped, divided
- ¼ cup mint leaves, roughly chopped, divided
- 1 pinch saffron threads
- 3 cloves
- 1 cinnamon stick
- 1 Tbsp vegetable oil

continued on page 242

Preheat the oven to 350°F. In a mixing bowl, combine rice with 3 cups of water and set aside. In a food processor or blender, purée garlic, ginger, lemon juice, yogurt, and cream. Set aside.

Place a large skillet over medium heat. Add the ghee or clarified butter. When it begins to shimmer, add onions, cumin, cayenne, paprika, pepper, garam masala, and turmeric, and sauté for 10-12 minutes, or until the onions are starting to brown. Add potato, cauliflower, carrots, and salt, and continue to sauté for 4-6 minutes, or until the potato begins to brown at the edges. Add tomato, jalapeño, French beans, peas, ¼ cup of the cilantro, and ⅛ cup of the mint, and continue to sauté for 3-4 minutes, or until the jalapeños begin to soften. Add garlic-ginger purée and sauté for an additional 3 minutes. Reduce the heat to low, cover the skillet, and allow it to simmer while you cook the rice.

In a separate pot, bring the 2 remaining cups of water, saffron, cloves, cinnamon, and vegetable oil to a boil over high heat. Reduce to low. Drain the soaking rice using a sieve or fine strainer and add it to the pot. Cover the pot and allow the rice to cook for 10 minutes. Discard the cloves and cinnamon stick.

Transfer the skillet contents to a baking dish in a single layer. Atop the vegetable mixture, layer the partially cooked rice. Cover the baking dish tightly with aluminum foil, transfer to the oven, and roast for 40-45 minutes or until the rice is fully cooked.

Remove the biryani from the oven and allow it to rest, covered for 15 minutes. Uncover the biryani, gently stir together the vegetable mixture with the rice, top with remaining cilantro and mint, and serve hot!

Nine Jewel Vegetable Pot
(Navratan Korma)

INDIA

TOTAL TIME: 1 hour, 25 minutes
CHARACTER: Main, Side
VESSEL: 9 x 13 inch baking dish, or equivalent
SERVES: 4–6

4 qt water
2 Tbsp + 1 tsp salt, divided
1 (about ½ lb) large russet potato, peeled, diced
½ head cauliflower, cut into small florets
1 cup fresh green peas
½ lb fresh green beans, diced
1 large red bell pepper
1 small carrot, diced
3 cloves garlic
1 inch fresh ginger, peeled
1 jalapeño pepper, stemmed
1 large tomato, diced
1 cup coconut cream
1 cup cashews, divided
3 Tbsp ghee or clarified butter
1 large onion, diced
1 tsp ground cumin
1 tsp ground coriander
1 tsp smoked paprika
1 tsp cayenne or other chile powder
1 tsp turmeric powder
1 tsp garam masala or other curry powder
½ cup golden raisins for garnish
½ cup pomegranate seeds for garnish

Preheat the oven to 350°F.

In a large pot, bring water to a boil over high heat, then reduce the heat to medium-low. Add 2 tablespoons of salt and potato, and simmer for 3 minutes. Add cauliflower, peas, green beans, bell pepper, and carrot, and simmer for an additional 3 minutes. Remove from heat and drain the vegetables in a colander. Set aside.

In a blender or food processor, purée the garlic, ginger, jalapeño, tomato, coconut cream, and ½ cup of the cashews.

Place a skillet over medium heat, and add the ghee or clarified butter. When it begins to shimmer, add the onion, cumin, coriander, paprika, cayenne, turmeric, garam masala, the remaining

continued on page 245

1 teaspoon of salt, and sauté for 6-8 minutes, or until the onions become translucent. Add the purée to the skillet, stir through, and bring the mixture to a boil. Remove from the heat.

In a baking dish, combine the partially cooked vegetables with the skillet contents and stir together evenly. Cover tightly with aluminum foil and transfer the baking dish to the oven. Braise the korma for 30-35 minutes, or until the vegetables are fully cooked.

Place a dry skillet over medium heat. Add the remaining ½ cup of cashews. Sauté for 3-4 minutes, stirring often, until the nuts are fragrant and slightly browned. In a food processor or in a zip top bag with a rolling pin, crush the toasted cashews. Remove the korma from the oven, garnish with raisins, pomegranate seeds, crushed cashews, and serve with naan bread or rice.

Curried Cauliflower and Potatoes
(Aloo Gobi)

INDIA

TOTAL TIME: 1 hour, 25 minutes
CHARACTER: Main, Side
VESSEL: 9 x 13 inch baking dish, or equivalent
SERVES: 4–6

2 (about 1 lb) large russet potatoes, peeled, cut into 1-inch pieces
1 head cauliflower, cut into large florets
2 Tbsp vegetable oil
2 tsp salt, divided
4 Tbsp ghee or clarified butter
1 Tbsp ground cumin
1 Tbsp ground coriander
1 Tbsp garam masala or other curry powder
1 tsp ground cinnamon
1 tsp turmeric powder
2 tsp cayenne or other chile powder
2 tsp ground black pepper
1 tsp sugar
4 cloves garlic, minced
1 can green chiles (hot or mild), diced
1 28-oz can puréed tomatoes
½ cup cilantro, divided
1 lime, juiced
Yogurt for garnish

Preheat the oven to 400°F. In a large mixing bowl, add potatoes, cauliflower, vegetable oil, and 1 teaspoon of salt. Toss until vegetables are evenly coated. Spread them out on a sheet pan and roast in the oven 35-40 minutes, or until they are beginning to brown at the edges. Toss the vegetables over once, halfway through the cooking.

While the vegetables are cooking, make the gravy. Place a skillet over medium-low heat, and add the ghee or clarified butter. When it begins to shimmer, add the cumin, coriander, curry powder, cinnamon, turmeric, chile powder, pepper, sugar, garlic, green chiles, and remaining 1 teaspoon of salt, and sauté until the garlic is very aromatic, but not darkened, about 2 minutes. Pour in the tomatoes and ¼ cup of the cilantro. Turn off the heat and stir to combine.

Reduce the oven to 350°F. Remove the roasted potatoes and cauliflower from the oven and transfer into a baking dish. Pour in the gravy and stir to combine thoroughly. Transfer the baking dish to the oven and roast uncovered for 20-25 minutes, or until the tomato sauce has thickened and coats the vegetables. Remove the aloo gobi from the oven and stir in lime juice. Garnish with the remaining cilantro and yogurt, and serve hot scoops with rice or naan bread.

Lamb Garlic Pilaf

(Plov)

UZBEKISTAN

TOTAL TIME: 2 hours, 20 minutes
CHARACTER: One Pot Meal, Main
VESSEL: 12 inch cast iron skillet with a lid, or other oven-safe skillet with a lid
SERVES: 4–6

Many years ago, I went on a whirlwind working tour of Central Asia. While I was in Kyrgyzstan, about to head to Uzbekistan, I had a rather unpleasant cafeteria meal at the American university there. When I was biting into an ill-advised, subpar "grilled cheese," hundreds of gunshots rang outside the window. *What?* At that time, there were vast social movements across Eastern Europe and they eventually spread to Central Asia . . . during my visit. Long story short, Kyrgyzstan was on lockdown and my visit to Uzbekistan was promptly cancelled. In honor of my *terrific* timing, I ate the national dish of Uzbekistan that night for dinner amidst a city-wide curfew.

—Howie

1 cup basmati or other long grain white rice
4 cups water, divided
¼ cup vegetable oil
1 lb lamb shoulder, diced
1½ tsp salt, divided
1 onion, thinly sliced half moons
½ lb carrots, cut into ¼ inch x 2 inch sticks
8 cloves garlic, lightly crushed
1 tbsp cumin
1 tsp ground black pepper

Preheat the oven to 350°F. In a mixing bowl, combine rice with 2 cups of water and set aside.

Place a skillet over medium heat and add the oil. When the oil begins to shimmer, add the lamb and 1 teaspoon salt and sauté, stirring often, until all of the meat has browned, about 6-8 minutes. Using a slotted spoon, remove the lamb to a plate and set aside.

Add onion to the skillet and sauté until the onion pieces have softened and begin to brown, about 8-10 minutes. Add carrots, garlic, cumin, and black pepper, and continue to sauté for an additional 6-8 minutes, or until the carrots have softened but not broken. Add the remaining 2 cups of water to the skillet and bring to a boil. Reduce the heat to low, add the browned lamb, cover, and simmer for 1 hour.

Turn off the heat and uncover the skillet. Drain the soaking rice and evenly distribute it across the top of the contents of the skillet. Sprinkle the remaining ½ teaspoon of salt across the top. Using the back of a spoon, make sure the rice is submerged in liquid, but do not mix it with the lamb mixture. Cover and transfer the skillet to the oven for 45 minutes.

Remove the skillet from the oven. Allow the plov to rest, covered, out of the oven for 15 minutes. Remove the lid, stir everything together, and serve directly to bowls.

Dessert!

S'Mread Pudding

USA

TOTAL TIME: 2 hours (or overnight, plus 1 hour)
CHARACTER: Dessert
VESSEL: 9 x 13 inch baking dish, or equivalent
SERVES: 6-8

> In our previous masterpiece on cast iron skillet recipes, *One Pan to Rule Them All*, Howie and I solved the essential problem with the ever-popular s'more. We wrap it in a tortilla, and there's no more mess! What could be better than getting all the good, gooey marshmallow, oozy chocolate, crunchy graham cracker, without the need to do laundry? I'll tell you what. Getting all that goodness without using your hands at all! We proudly present the total package, the S'Mread Pudding!
>
> —Greg

5 cups (about 1 lb) brioche bread, cut into 1-inch cubes
5 eggs
2 cups half-and-half or milk
3 Tbsp sugar
1 tsp salt
1 tsp vanilla extract
5 oz (1 sleeve) graham crackers
2 Tbsp butter, divided
6 oz (half a bag) milk chocolate chips
8 oz (half a bag) mini marshmallows
Ice cream for serving

Preheat oven to 375°F. Place bread cubes on a sheet pan and toast for 10-15 minutes. You know what toast looks like!

In a blender, combine eggs, half-and-half or milk, sugar, salt, vanilla, and graham crackers, and blend until smooth.

Smear 1 tablespoon of butter across the bottom and sides of a baking dish. Place half of the bread pieces into the baking dish, in a single layer. Atop the bread, layer half of the chocolate chips and half of the marshmallows. Repeat the layers with the second half of bread, chocolate chips, and marshmallows.

Slowly pour the egg mixture evenly over, being sure that some of the liquid reaches most, if not all, of the bread. Use the back of a wooden spoon, a clean hand, or spatula, to compress the whole mixture to ensure that the liquid is evenly distributed. Cover with plastic wrap and set aside for at least one hour (or in the refrigerator overnight).

Uncover and dot the top with pinches of the remaining butter. Transfer the baking dish to the center rack of the oven. Bake for 30-35 minutes, or until the top begins to brown and get crusty.

Remove the casserole from the oven, scoop hot servings with an oversized spoon! Add in some ice cream and enjoy.

Bourbon White Chocolate Pistachio Bread Pudding

USA

TOTAL TIME: 2 hours (or overnight, plus 1 hour)
CHARACTER: Dessert
VESSEL: 9 x 13 inch baking dish, or equivalent
SERVES: 6–8

This one time, in China . . . *Hold on, we know where this is going!* No, you hold on! This one time in China, we met this local guy who adopted the English name "White Chocolate," as he was a huge fan of NBA star Jason Williams. We spent an entertaining evening on the banks of the Tuo River watching boats, munching on pistachios, and sipping expensive bourbon. See. You had no idea.

—Greg

BREAD PUDDING:

5 eggs
3 cups half-and-half or cream
¼ cup brown sugar, packed
4 Tbsp bourbon whiskey
1 tsp salt
1 tsp vanilla extract
1 Tbsp butter
5 cups (about 1 lb) crusty bread, cut into 1-inch pieces
1 cup white chocolate chips
1 cup pistachios, shelled

BOURBON SAUCE:

8 Tbsp (1 stick) butter
1 cup sugar
½ tsp salt
¼ cup heavy cream
¼ cup bourbon whiskey

In a large mixing bowl, whisk together eggs, half-and-half or cream, brown sugar, bourbon, salt, and vanilla.

Smear butter across the bottom and sides of a baking dish. Place half of the bread pieces into the baking dish. Be sure you have one even layer with a flat top (no bread hills).
Sprinkle chocolate chips and pistachios across the top of the bread. Scatter the remaining bread in another layer, followed by the remaining chocolate and pistachios.

continued on page 256

Slowly pour the egg mixture evenly over the bread mixture, being sure that some of the liquid reaches most, if not all, of the bread. Use the back of a wooden spoon, a clean hand, or spatula, to compress the whole mixture to ensure that the liquid is evenly distributed.

Cover with plastic wrap and set aside for at least 1 hour (or in the refrigerator overnight).

Preheat the oven to 375°F. Uncover the baking dish and transfer to the center rack of the oven. Bake for 40-45 minutes, or until the top is beginning to brown and get crusty. If the top has browned before 40 minutes is up, loosely place aluminum foil across the top of the baking dish for the remainder of time.

To make the sauce, melt butter in a skillet over medium heat. Add sugar and salt, and stir until the sugar is dissolved, about 3 minutes. Stir in the cream and bourbon, and bring the mixture to a boil, then reduce the heat to low. Simmer the sauce for 10 minutes, turn off the heat, and set aside until the bread pudding is to be served.

Remove the bread pudding from the oven, and scoop hot servings with an oversized spoon! Dress with bourbon sauce and enjoy!

Salted Caramel Apple Crisp

USA

TOTAL TIME: 1 hour
CHARACTER: Dessert
VESSEL: 9 x 13 inch baking dish, or equivalent
SERVES: 6-8

> My lovely wife, Jessica, is the pastry chef in our house. With two dessert-obsessed sons, you can guess who earns the gold star in our family! Her *rock star* take on a humble apple crisp has rapidly become an undeniable Thanksgiving staple. Well, at least it used to be just for Thanksgiving. Nowadays, I think we're up to every other Thursday.
>
> —Howie

FILLING:

6 large Granny Smith or other tart apples, peeled, diced
3 Tbsp granulated sugar
3 Tbsp brown sugar
2 tsp ground cinnamon
½ tsp salt
8 traditional caramel candies (the non-hard type)
1 Tbsp heavy cream

TOPPING:

¾ cup whole wheat flour
½ tsp cinnamon
⅓ cup granulated sugar
⅓ cup brown sugar
¾ cup unsalted butter, cold, cut into ½ inch cubes
¾ cup rolled oats

DRIZZLE:

10 traditional caramel candies (the non-hard type)
1 tsp water
½ tsp salt
1 Tbsp unsalted butter

Preheat the oven to 375°F. In a large mixing bowl, Mix apples, granulated sugar, brown sugar, cinnamon, and salt. Set aside.

To make the topping, in the bowl of a food processor, combine flour, cinnamon, sugar, brown sugar, and pulse 5-6 times. Add half of the butter and pulse 5-6 times to combine. Occasionally use a spoon to ensure that the ingredients are being mixed evenly. Add the remaining butter and

continued on page 259

pulse 5-6 more times. Pour contents into a mixing bowl. Add oats and mix with clean hands until topping resembles coarse crumbs.

Pour apple mixture into a baking dish. Place 8 caramels and heavy cream in a microwave-safe bowl and melt on 50% power in the microwave in 30-second increments until melted. Drizzle the melted caramels over the apple mixture. Evenly distribute the topping on the apple mixture. Transfer the baking dish to the oven and bake for 30-45 minutes, or until topping is golden brown and apples are tender.

When the casserole has cooled, make the caramel drizzle for the top. Mix 10 caramels, water, salt, and butter in a microwave-safe bowl. Heat this mixture in the microwave on high in 30 second increments until melted. Drizzle over top of the crisp or on individual servings. Serve with vanilla ice cream.

Lemon Blueberry Cobbler

USA

TOTAL TIME: 1 hour
CHARACTER: Dessert
VESSEL: 8 x 8 inch baking dish, or equivalent
SERVES: 6-8

> A cobbler makes shoes. Shoes make the man. Man made fire. Fire creates ashes. Ashes fertilize soil. Soil bears trees. Trees produce fruit. Baked fruit needs a hat, but was mistakenly sent to the cobbler. Now, does the name make sense? In my dreams.
>
> —Greg

FILLING:

24 oz frozen blueberries
¾ cup granulated sugar
3 Tbsp lemon juice (1 large lemon)
1 tsp lemon zest, firmly packed
2 Tbsp tapioca starch

TOPPING:

1 cup flour
1 tsp baking powder
¼ tsp salt
1 tsp lemon zest, firmly packed
2 Tbsp granulated sugar, divided
6 Tbsp unsalted butter, cold, cut into ½ inch cubes
3/8 cup buttermilk

Preheat the oven to 400°F.

In a mixing bowl, combine blueberries, sugar, lemon juice, lemon zest, and tapioca starch. Pour the mixture into a baking dish. Transfer the baking dish to the oven and bake for 15 minutes. Stir halfway through to ensure berries are evenly warmed.

While the berry mixture is warming, make the topping. In a large mixing bowl, whisk together flour, baking powder, salt, lemon zest, and 1 tablespoon of sugar. Add the butter cubes and incorporate into the flour mixture with a pastry cutter or squeeze with your fingertips until the pieces of butter are consistently smaller than peas. Add buttermilk and knead with your hands until a consistent dough forms.

Remove berry mixture from the oven. Form 9 free-form biscuits from the dough and place evenly atop the berry mixture in the baking dish. Sprinkle the remaining 1 tablespoon of sugar atop the biscuit dough. Transfer the baking dish to the oven and bake for an additional 20-25 minutes, or until the topping is golden brown. Remove the cobbler from the oven and serve warm with ice cream or whipped cream.

Banana Dream Casserole

USA

TOTAL TIME: 1 hour, 30 minutes
CHARACTER: Dessert
VESSEL: 9 x 13 inch baking dish, or equivalent
SERVES: 6-8

> When I was a kid, I was a huge fan of *Gilligan's Island*. Hilarious hijinks in the tropics kept me coming back for more. Actually, truth be told, it was Mary Ann. I adored a down-home girl, cute pigtails, and of course, she was constantly making her dreamy coconut cream pies. Mary Ann, all the way! But coconuts are really hard to crack. So, here's a casserole-ified banana version . . . with absolutely no Ginger.
>
> —Greg

FILLING:

2½ cups milk
1 cup sugar
4 Tbsp cornstarch
½ tsp salt
4 egg yolks (keep yolks and whites in separate bowls)
3 Tbsp unsalted butter
1½ tsp vanilla extract
3 medium bananas, cut into ½ inch slices

CRUST:

2 cups (about 1½ sleeves) graham crackers, finely ground
2 Tbsp sugar
9 Tbsp butter, melted

MERINGUE TOPPING:

4 egg whites
½ tsp cream of tartar
1 tsp vanilla extract
½ cup sugar

To prepare filling, in a heavy bottomed saucepan, whisk together milk, sugar, cornstarch, and salt. Cook milk mixture over medium-low heat until the mixture boils and thickens, whisking constantly to avoid scalding the milk. Once the mixture boils, cook 2 more minutes.

Move mixture off heat briefly and spoon half a cup of the hot milk mixture into the egg yolks and stir well. Stir this egg yolk mixture into the saucepan and put back on the heat for 2 more minutes to thicken more. Pour the mixture into a mixing bowl to cool. Add butter and vanilla and stir until butter has melted and vanilla is fully incorporated. Place plastic wrap directly on the surface of the custard (to keep a film from forming) and cool for an hour.

Preheat the oven to 350°F.

To make the crust, in a mixing bowl, combine graham cracker crumbs, sugar, and melted butter. Butter a baking dish. Press graham cracker crumb mix into the bottom of the baking dish evenly. Bake for 10 minutes until golden. Remove the crust from the oven and set aside to cool.

To prepare the meringue topping, whip egg whites, cream of tartar, and vanilla in a stand mixer on high speed until soft peaks form. Slowly add sugar and continue to whip until stiff peaks form.

To assemble the casserole, spread a small amount of custard on the crust evenly (½ inch layer). Spread sliced bananas in one even layer over the custard edge to edge. Gently pour in remaining custard and spread evenly in the pan. Drop meringue gently on top of the custard and spread evenly, sealing the edges.

Transfer the baking dish to the oven and bake for 10-12 minutes, or until the meringue begins to brown on the edges. Remove the casserole from the oven and serve hot, dreamy scoops.

Rocky Road Pie

USA

TOTAL TIME: 30 minutes
CHARACTER: Dessert
VESSEL: 8 x 8 inch baking dish, or equivalent
SERVES: 4-6

I scream. You scream. We all scream for ice cream! Rocky road is an American favorite that dates back, according to some stories, as far as 1906. Where the combination of chocolate, marshmallows, and almonds can be arguably traced to that time, the name "rocky road" rings most authentic when ice cream magnates in the late 1920s wanted to make America feel a bit better after the stock market crash of 1929. *We've all been on a rocky road, so sweeten up life with this treat.* We all need a little boost now and again and here's our solution that won't melt!

—Howie

Butter for coating the baking dish

17 chocolate sandwich cookies, filling removed (We prefer the brand that starts with "Ore...")

¼ cup sugar

6 Tbsp unsalted butter, melted

½ cup unsalted almonds, slivered or chopped

½ cup milk chocolate chips or chopped milk chocolate

½ cup bittersweet chocolate chips or chopped bittersweet chocolate

5 oz miniature marshmallows

Preheat the oven to 375°F.

Butter the inside of a baking dish. Line with parchment paper and trim so it comes up two opposite sides, slightly draping over the edges.

Using a food processor or a zip top bag with a rolling pin, process cookies into fine crumbs. Combine with sugar and melted butter until evenly mixed. Press the mixture firmly into the bottom and sides of the dish to make an even crust. Transfer to the oven and bake for 10 minutes. Remove the cookie crust from the oven.

Layer half of the almonds, chocolate chips, and marshmallows onto the crust. Repeat with the remaining almonds, chips, and marshmallows. Try to keep the marshmallows away from edges of the pan to avoid them sticking. Return the baking dish to the oven and bake for 8-10 minutes, or until the marshmallows are golden in color.

Remove the pie from the oven and let it cool completely. Using the parchment paper on two sides, remove the pie from the baking dish and slice into bars.

Cannoli-fied Tiramisu

ITALY/USA

TOTAL TIME: 1 hour, 45 minutes
CHARACTER: Dessert
VESSEL: 8 x 8 inch baking dish, or equivalent
SERVES: 4-6

> I understand that you've just had an amazing Italian meal from the Europe chapter of this book. But now you just can't decide between cannoli and tiramisu for dessert. So, don't.
>
> —Greg

3 cups whole-milk ricotta
1 cup heavy whipping cream
1 cup confectioners' sugar
1 tsp vanilla extract
2 tsp powdered instant coffee
⅓ cup miniature chocolate chips
32 vanilla wafer cookies (We prefer the brand with the first two letters of "vanilla" deleted)

Place the bowl of a stand mixer and the accompanying whisk attachment in the refrigerator to chill for 30 minutes.

Drain ricotta through cheesecloth or a nut milk bag to remove excess liquid. In the chilled mixing bowl, combine the ricotta, whipping cream, and confectioners' sugar, and whisk in the stand mixer for 3-4 minutes, or until thick. Add vanilla and instant coffee and whisk until well incorporated. Remove the bowl from the mixer and stir in chocolate chips.

Spread a third of the creamy filling evenly in a baking dish. Atop the filling, place 16 wafer cookies in 4 rows of 4. Evenly spread another layer using a third of the filling. Repeat a layer of the cookies. Spread the remaining filling on top, using a spatula or the back of a spoon to smooth the top.

Cover with plastic wrap and chill the cannoli-fied tiramisu in refrigerator for at least an hour before serving creamy scoops. After about 12 hours in the fridge, the wafer cookies begin to *disappear*, so don't wait so long!

Deep Dessert Pancake
(Pannu Kakkau)

FINLAND

TOTAL TIME: 1 hour
CHARACTER: Dessert
VESSEL: 9 x 13 inch baking dish, or equivalent
SERVES: 10-12

> I have never been to Finland. But I have been to my office. One day, at my office, Pia, my Finnish coworker (who, coincidentally, has been to Finland), was talking about Finnish food. I was concerned about finishing this book, so I asked her for her favorite Finnish casserole. It was so good, I nearly finished it in one sitting.
>
> —Greg

PANNU KAKKAU:

6 Tbsp butter
1 cup flour
1 cup granulated sugar
4 eggs
2 cups whole milk
1 tsp vanilla extract

WHIPPED CREAM:

2 cups cream
1½ tsp vanilla extract
3 Tbsp sugar
Strawberries, sliced for serving

Preheat the oven to 350°F.

Place the butter in the baking dish, and put it in the oven to melt. Allow butter to cook until it is lightly bubbling, about 5 minutes.

While the butter is melting, combine the flour, sugar, eggs, milk, and vanilla in a large bowl. With a whisk or electric beater, beat well until completely combined and frothy on the top, about 3 minutes. The batter will be very loose—looser than your typical pancake batter.

Carefully remove the baking dish from the oven and swish the melted butter to coat the sides of the pan. Gently pour the batter into the middle of the pan, and return it to the oven. Cook for 40-50 minutes, until the top is lightly brown. When it is done, the middle will still lightly jiggle.

When the pancake is nearly done, prepare the whipped cream by combining the cream, vanilla, and sugar in a large bowl. Beat with an electric mixer until the cream forms soft peaks, about 3 minutes.

Serve the pancake while hot, with strawberries and whipped cream.

ABOUT THE AUTHORS

Greg Matza and Howie Southworth are the best-selling team behind *One Pan to Rule Them All: 100 Cast-Iron Skillet Recipes for Indoors and Out*.

They first formed their creative partnership more than twenty-five years ago. This dynamic duo first met during college, working at a summer camp on the University of California campus in Santa Barbara. Be jealous. They became fast friends over Sammy Davis Jr. tunes, Freebirds burritos, and cans of Cactus Cooler.

Their early collaborations included amateur theater productions, ill-fated double-dates, harrowing road trips, and epic dinner parties. These soirees were the seed of their culinary partnership, and continue to this day. Weeks are spent devising and preparing themed parties, which have ranged from A Pirate Feast to a 20-Course Chinese Banquet. Their dress code simply reads, "elastic."

When not near their stoves, Howie and Greg can likely be found eating their way across China. For this insatiable pair, going out for some Sichuan usually involves a trans-Pacific flight. Want to share in their culinary adventures? Visit them on Instagram and Twitter @HowieAndGreg.

INDEX

C

T

U

V

W

Y

Z

CONVERSION CHARTS

METRIC AND IMPERIAL CONVERSIONS
(These conversions are rounded for convenience)

Ingredient	Cups/Tablespoons/ Teaspoons	Ounces	Grams/Milliliters
Butter	1 cup = 16 tablespoons = 2 sticks	8 ounces	230 grams
Cheese, shredded	1 cup	4 ounces	110 grams
Cream cheese	1 tablespoon	0.5 ounce	14.5 grams
Cornstarch	1 tablespoon	0.3 ounce	8 grams
Flour, all-purpose	1 cup/1 tablespoon	4.5 ounces/0.3 ounce	125 grams/8 grams
Flour, whole wheat	1 cup	4 ounces	120 grams
Fruit, dried	1 cup	4 ounces	120 grams
Fruits or veggies, chopped	1 cup	5 to 7 ounces	145 to 200 grams
Fruits or veggies, pureed	1 cup	8.5 ounces	245 grams
Honey, maple syrup, or corn syrup	1 tablespoon	.75 ounce	20 grams
Liquids: cream, milk, water, or juice	1 cup	8 fluid ounces	240 milliliters
Oats	1 cup	5.5 ounces	150 grams
Salt	1 teaspoon	0.2 ounce	6 grams
Spices: cinnamon, cloves, ginger, or nutmeg (ground)	1 teaspoon	0.2 ounce	5 milliliters
Sugar, brown, firmly packed	1 cup	7 ounces	200 grams
Sugar, white	1 cup/1 tablespoon	7 ounces/0.5 ounce	200 grams/12.5 grams
Vanilla extract	1 teaspoon	0.2 ounce	4 grams

OVEN TEMPERATURES

Fahrenheit	Celsius	Gas Mark
225°	110°	¼
250°	120°	½
275°	140°	1
300°	150°	2
325°	160°	3
350°	180°	4
375°	190°	5
400°	200°	6
425°	220°	7
450°	230°	8